EASY GUITAR
WITH NOTES & TAB

CELTIC CLASSICS

ISBN 978-1-4584-4078-5

HAL•LEONARD®
CORPORATION
7777 W. BLUEMOUND RD. P.O. BOX 13819 MILWAUKEE, WI 53213

In Australia Contact:
Hal Leonard Australia Pty. Ltd.
4 Lentara Court
Cheltenham, Victoria, 3192 Australia
Email: ausadmin@halleonard.com.au

Visit Hal Leonard Online at
www.halleonard.com

STRUM AND PICK PATTERNS

This chart contains the suggested strum and pick patterns that are referred to by number at the beginning of each song in this book. The symbols ⊓ and ∨ in the strum patterns refer to down and up strokes, respectively. The letters in the pick patterns indicate which right-hand fingers play which strings.

p = thumb
i = index finger
m = middle finger
a = ring finger

For example; Pick Pattern 2
is played: thumb - index - middle - ring

Strum Patterns   ## Pick Patterns

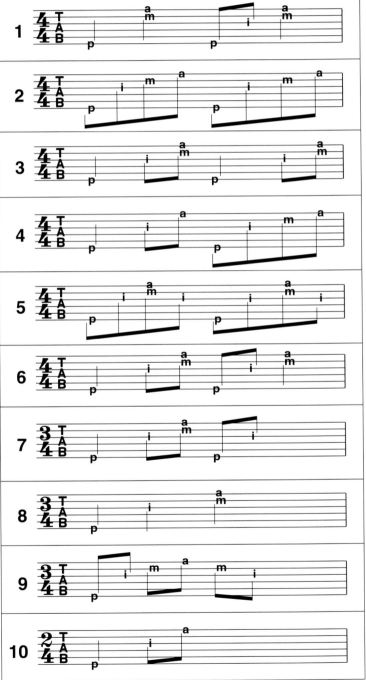

You can use the 3/4 Strum and Pick Patterns in songs written in compound meter (6/8, 9/8, 12/8, etc.). For example, you can accompany a song in 6/8 by playing the 3/4 pattern twice in each measure. The 4/4 Strum and Pick Patterns can be used for songs written in cut time (¢) by doubling the note time values in the patterns. Each pattern would therefore last two measures in cut time.

Be Thou My Vision

Traditional Irish
Translated by Mary E. Byrne

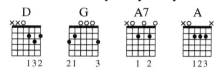

Strum Pattern: 8
Pick Pattern: 8

Verse
Moderately

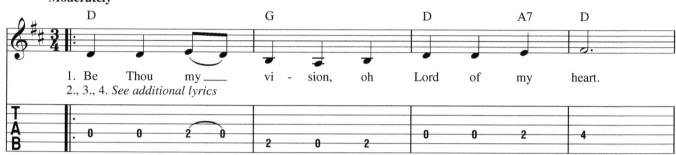

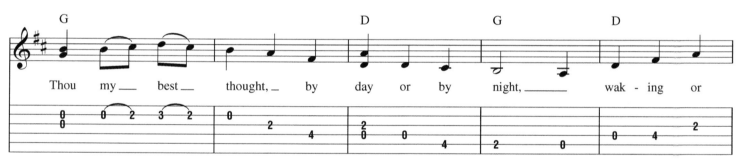

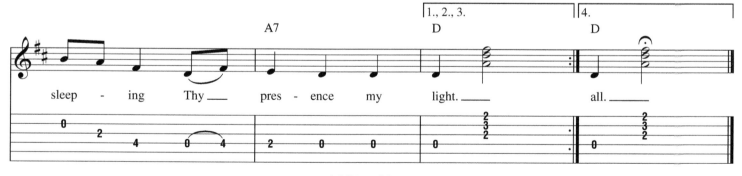

Additional Lyrics

2. Be Thou my wisdom, and Thou my true word.
   I ever with Thee and Thou with me, Lord.
   Thou my great Father, I Thy true son,
   Thou in me dwelling, and I with Thee one.

3. Riches I heed not, nor man's empty praise.
   Thou mine inheritance, now and always.
   Thou and Thou only, first in my heart,
   High King of heaven, my treasure Thou art.

4. High King of heaven, my victory won.
   May I reach heaven's joys, oh bright heav'n's sun!
   Heart of my own heart, whatever befall,
   Still be my vision, oh Ruler of all.

Believe Me, If All Those Endearing Young Charms

Words and Music by Thomas Moore

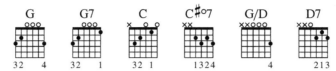

Strum Pattern: 7
Pick Pattern: 7

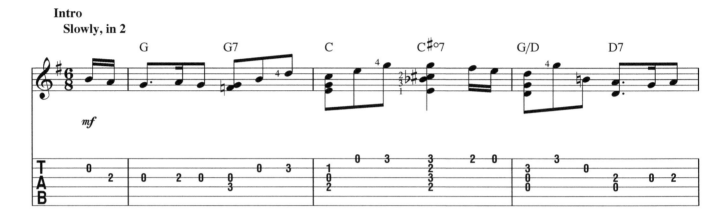

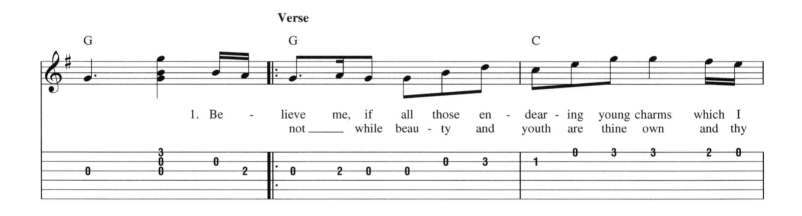

1. Be - lieve me, if all those en - dear - ing young charms which I
not while beau - ty and youth are thine own and thy

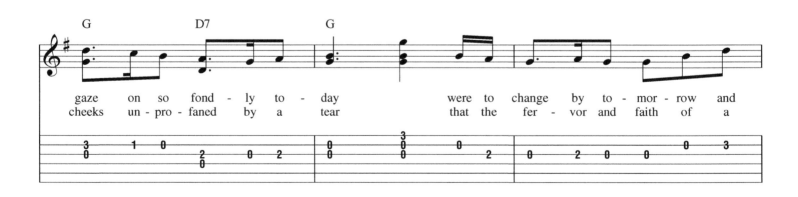

gaze on so fond - ly to - day
cheeks un - pro - faned by a tear
were to change by to - mor - row and
that the fer - vor and faith of a

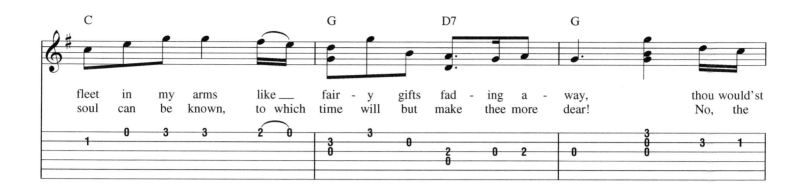

fleet in my arms like__ fair - y gifts fad - ing a - way, thou would'st
soul can be known, to which time will but make thee more dear! No, the

still be a - dored as this mo - ment thou art. Let thy love - li - ness fade as it
heart that has tru - ly loved nev - er for - gets, but as tru - ly, loves on to the

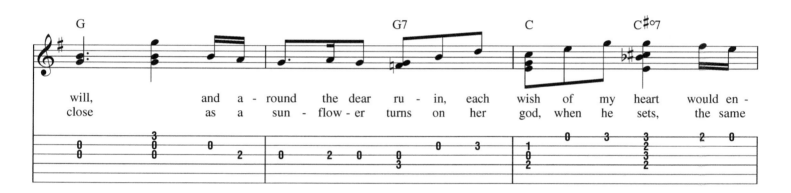

will, and a - round the dear ru - in, each wish of my heart would en -
close as a sun - flow - er turns on her god, when he sets, the same

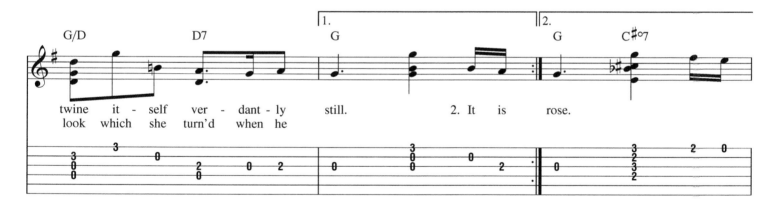

twine it - self ver - dant - ly still. 2. It is rose.
look which she turn'd when he

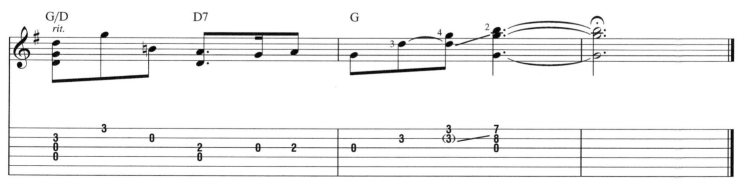

Bendemeer's Stream

Traditional Irish Folk Melody
Lyrics by Thomas Moore

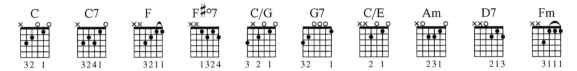

Strum Pattern: 8
Pick Pattern: 8

Intro
Moderately

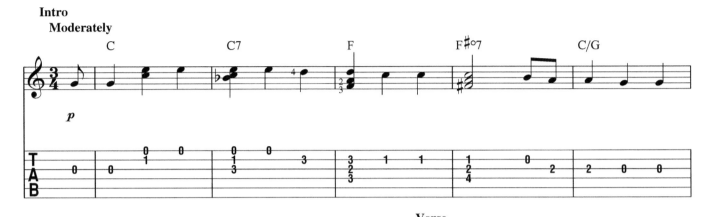

Verse

1. There's a bow - er of ros - es by
   ros - es soon with - ered that

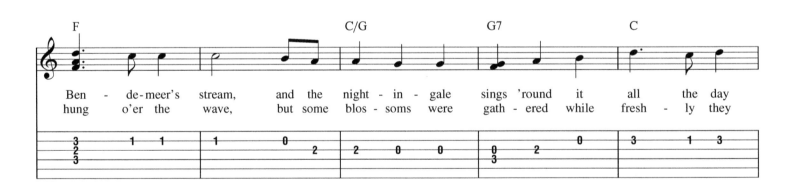

Ben - de-meer's stream, and the night - in - gale sings 'round it all the day
hung o'er the wave, but some blos - soms were gath - ered while fresh - ly they

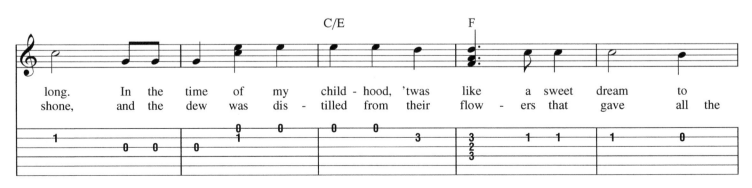

long. In the time of my child - hood, 'twas like a sweet dream to
shone, and the dew was dis - tilled from their flow - ers that gave all the

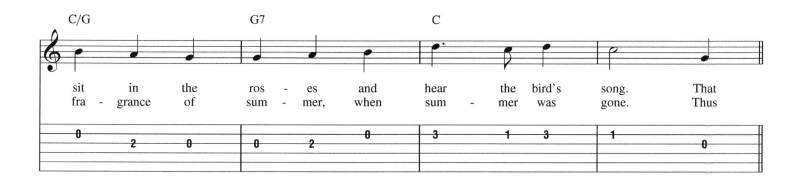

sit in the ros - es and hear the bird's song. That
fra - grance of sum - mer, when sum - mer was gone. Thus

Bridge

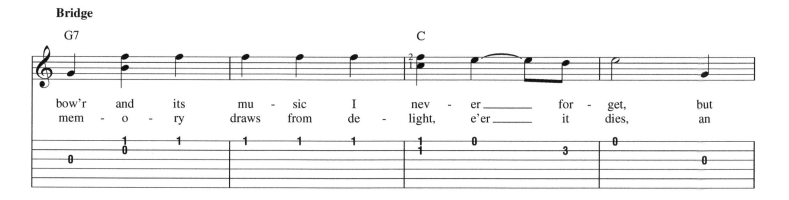

bow'r and its mu - sic I nev - er _____ for - get, but
mem - o - ry draws from de - light, e'er _____ it dies, an

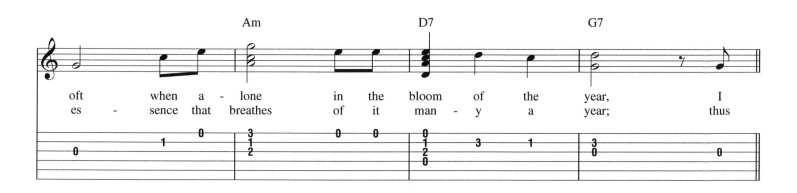

oft when a - lone in the bloom of the year, I
es - sence that breathes of it man - y a year; thus

Outro

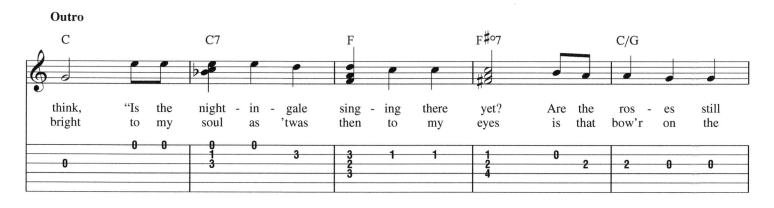

think, "Is the night - in - gale sing - ing there yet? Are the ros - es still
bright to my soul as 'twas then to my eyes is that bow'r on the

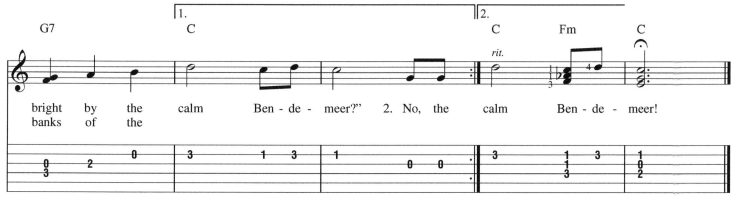

bright by the calm Ben - de - meer?" 2. No, the calm Ben - de - meer!
banks of the

7

The Bluebells of Scotland

Traditional

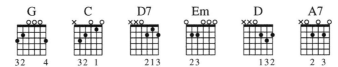

Strum Pattern: 3
Pick Pattern: 3

Verse
Moderately

1. Oh, where, tell me where is your __ High - land lad - die gone? Oh,
   where, tell me where did your __ High - land lad - die dwell? Oh,
   what, tell me what does your __ High - land lad - die wear? Oh,

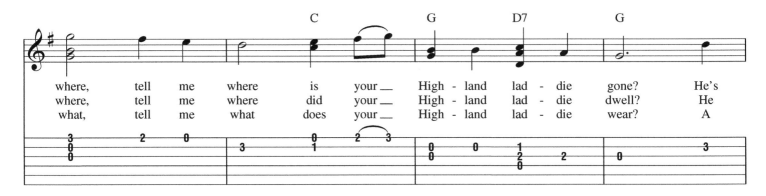

where, tell me where is your __ High - land lad - die gone? He's
where, tell me where did your __ High - land lad - die dwell? He
what, tell me what does your __ High - land lad - die wear? A

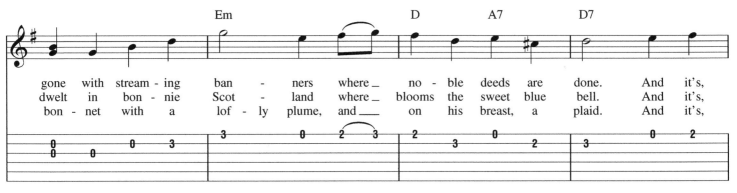

gone with stream - ing ban - ners where __ no - ble deeds are done. And it's,
dwelt in bon - nie Scot - land where __ blooms the sweet blue bell. And it's,
bon - net with a lof - ly plume, and __ on his breast, a plaid. And it's,

oh, in my heart I _____ wish him safe at home. 2. Oh, lad.
oh, in my heart I _____ lo'e my lad - die well. 3. Oh,
oh, in my heart I _____ lo'e my High - land

Has Sorrow Thy Young Days Shaded?

Traditional

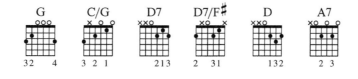

Strum Pattern: 7
Pick Pattern: 7

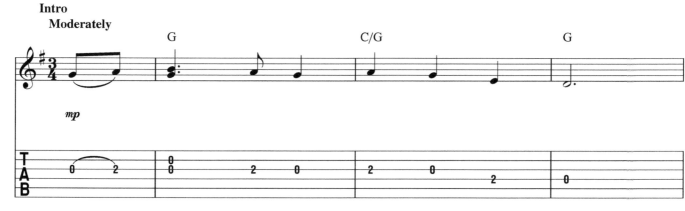

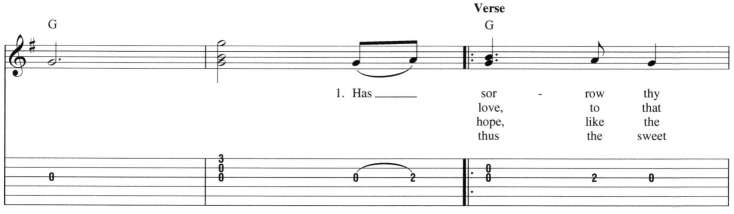

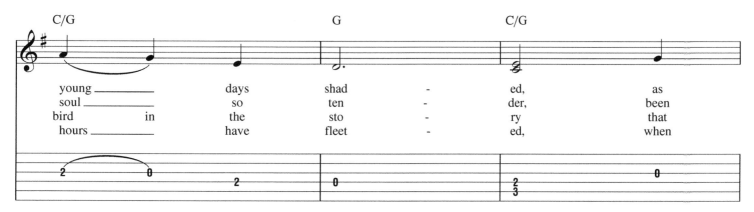

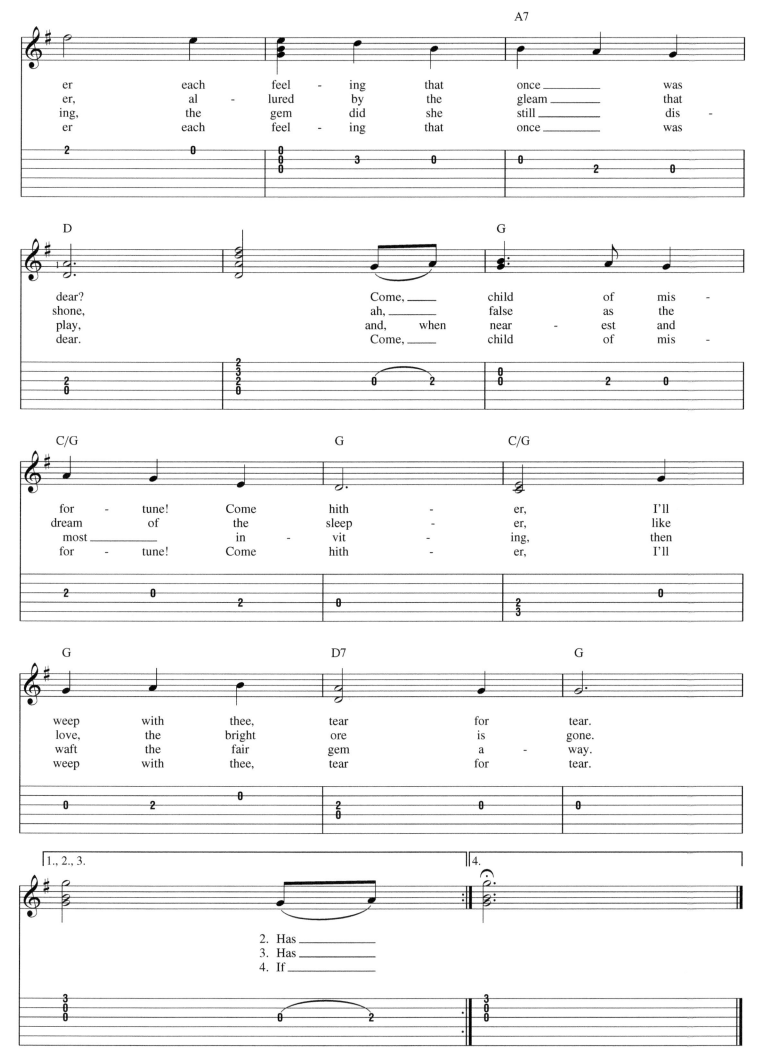

A Bunch of Thyme

Traditional Irish Folk Song

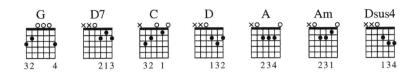

Strum Pattern: 4
Pick Pattern: 4

Intro
Moderately

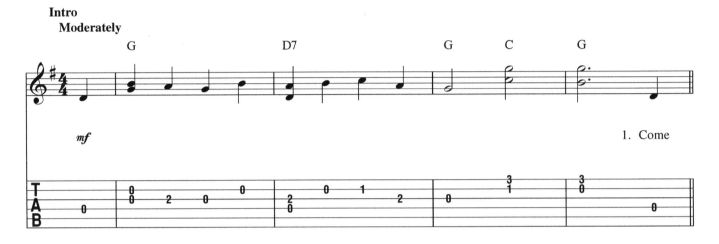

1. Come

Verse

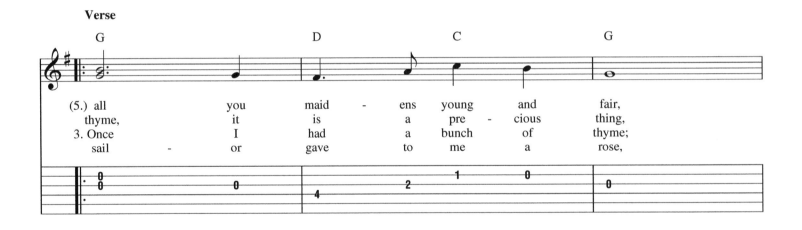

(5.) all you maid - ens young and fair,
thyme, it is a pre - cious thing,
3. Once I had a bunch of thyme;
sail - or gave to me a rose,

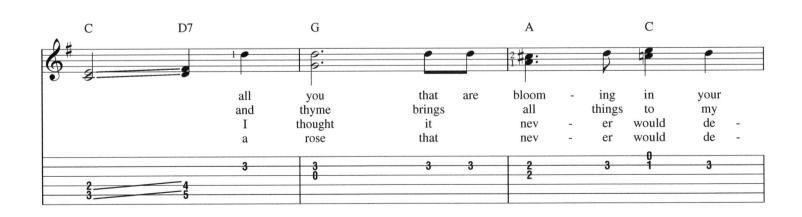

all you that are bloom - ing in your
and thyme brings all things to my
I thought it nev - er would de -
a rose that nev - er would de -

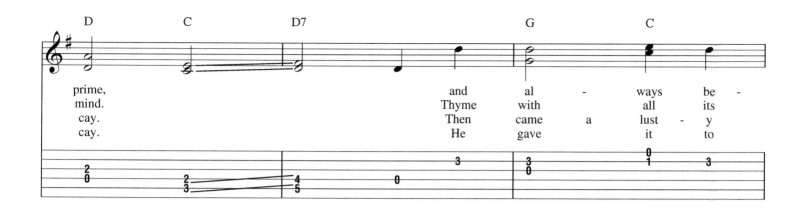

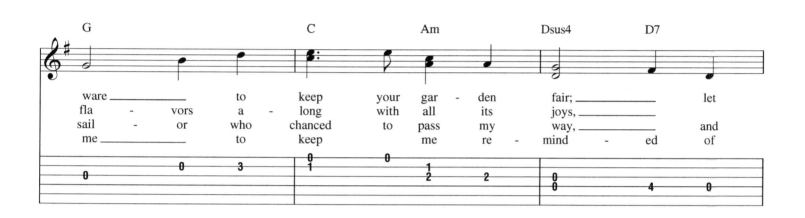

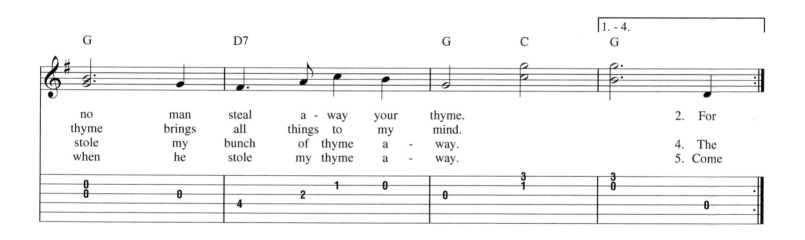

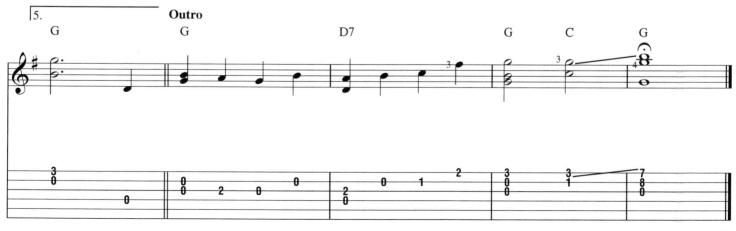

Carrickfergus

Traditional Irish Folk Song

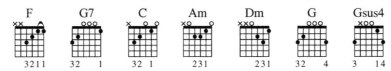

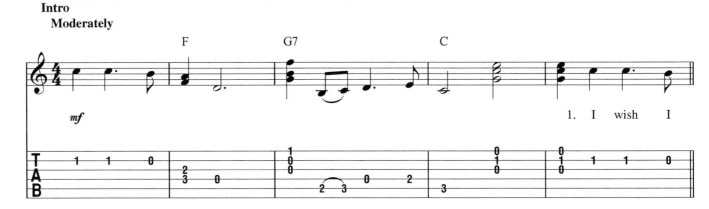

Strum Pattern: 3
Pick Pattern: 3

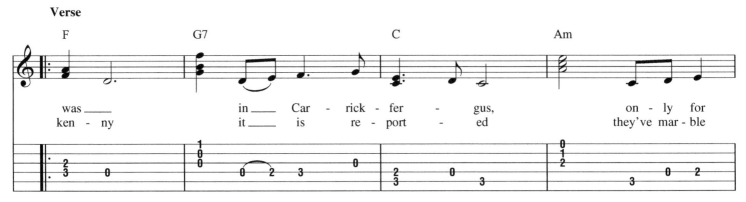

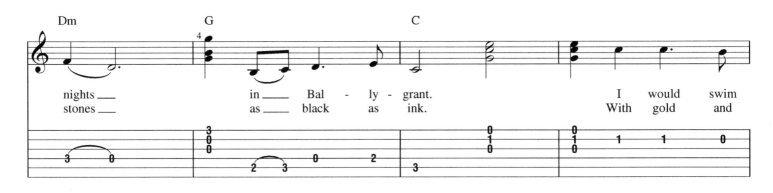

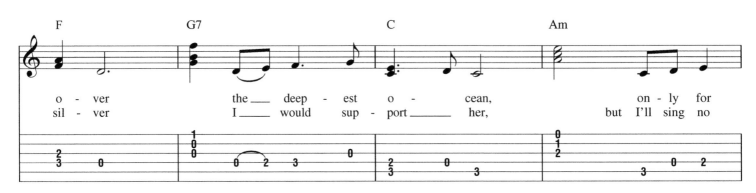

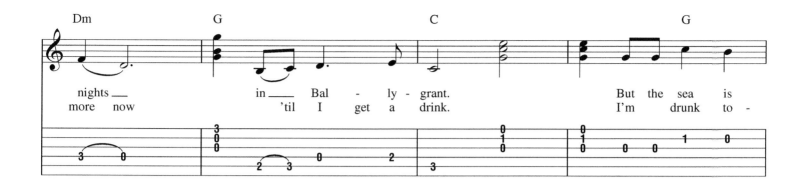

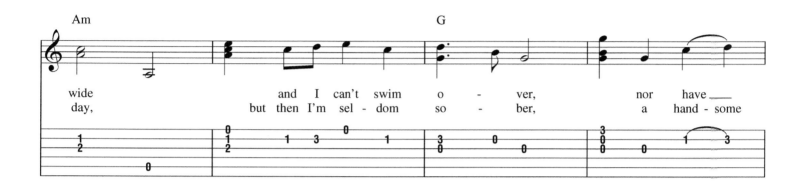

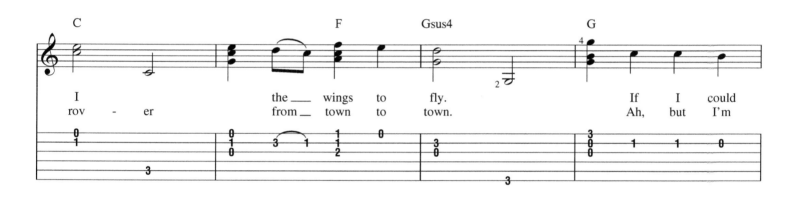

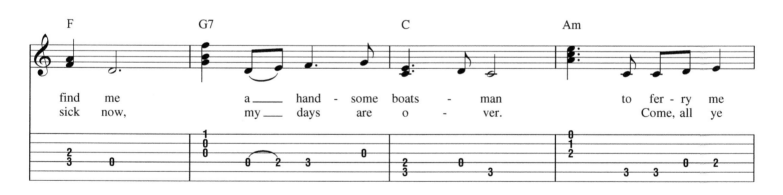

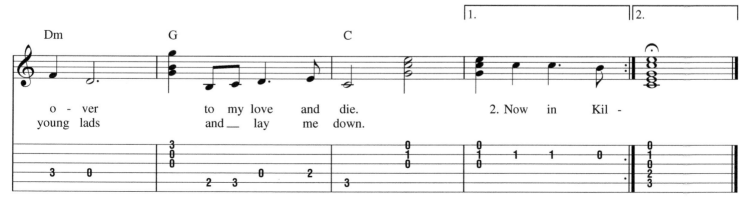

The Croppy Boy

Eighteenth Century Irish Folk Song

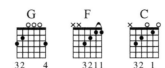

Strum Pattern: 8
Pick Pattern: 8

Additional Lyrics

4. As I was passing my father's door, my brother William stood at the door.
   My aged father stood there also, my tender mother, her hair she tore.

5 As I was going up Wexford Hill, who could blame me to cry my fill?
   I looked behind and I looked before, my aged mother I shall see no more.

6. As I was mounted on the scaffold high, my aged father was standing by.
   My aged father did me deny, and the name he gave me was the croppy boy.

7. 'Twas in the Dungannon this young man died, and in Dungannon his body lies.
   And you good people that do pass by, oh, shed a tear for the croppy boy.

Down by the Sally Gardens

Poem by William Butler Yeats
Music from Irish air "The Maids of Mourne Shore," arranged by Herbert Hughes

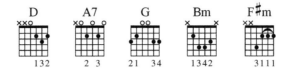

Strum Pattern: 3
Pick Pattern: 3

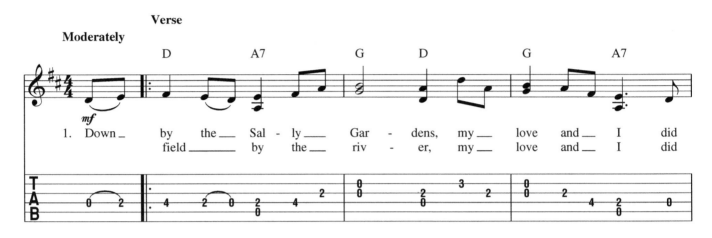

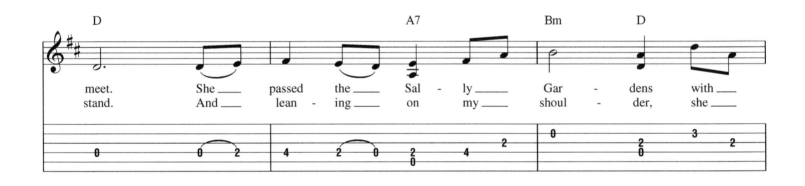

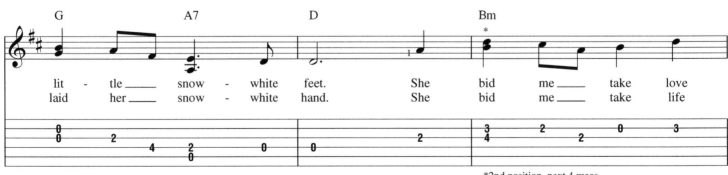

*2nd position, next 4 meas.

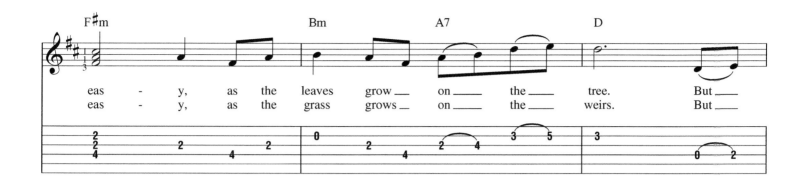

eas - y, as the leaves grow __ on __ the __ tree. But __
eas - y, as the grass grows __ on __ the __ weirs. But __

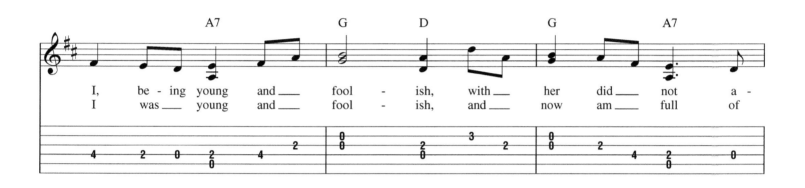

I, be - ing young and __ fool - ish, with __ her did __ not a -
I was __ young and __ fool - ish, and __ now am __ full of

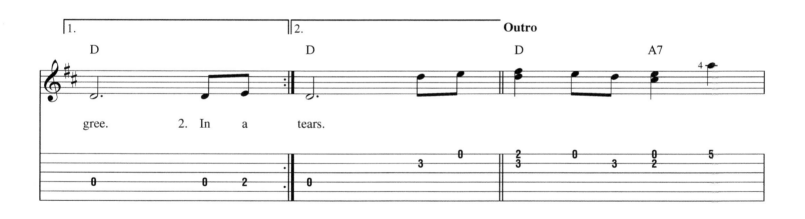

1. 2. **Outro**

gree. 2. In a tears.

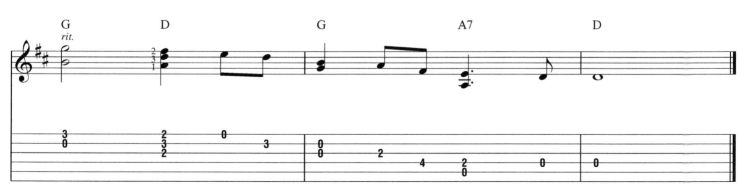

rit.

Finnegan's Wake

Traditional Irish Folk Song

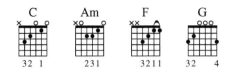

Strum Pattern: 3
Pick Pattern: 3

Verse
Moderately, in 2

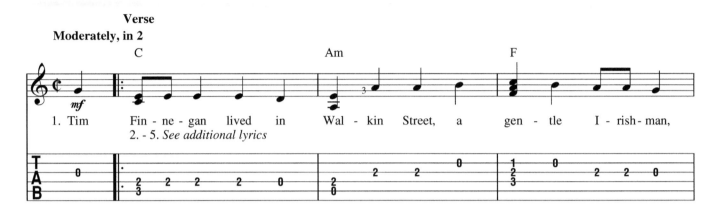

1. Tim Fin - ne - gan lived in Wal - kin Street, a gen - tle I - rish - man,
2. - 5. *See additional lyrics*

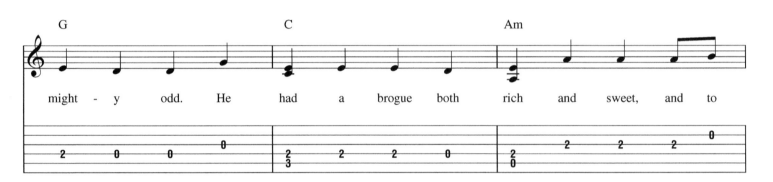

might - y odd. He had a brogue both rich and sweet, and to

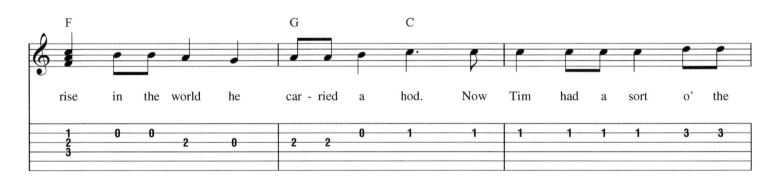

rise in the world he car - ried a hod. Now Tim had a sort o' the

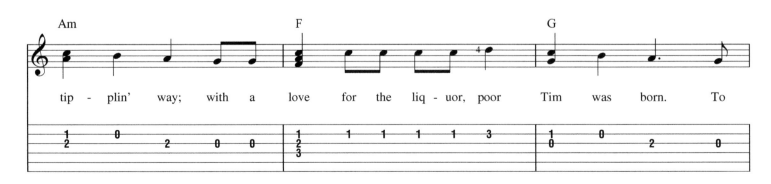

tip - plin' way; with a love for the liq - uor, poor Tim was born. To

Additional Lyrics

2. One mornin', Tim was rather full;
His head felt heavy, which made him shake.
He fell from a ladder and broke his skull,
And they carried him home, his corpse to wake.
They rolled him up in a nice clean sheet
And laid him out upon the bed;
A gallon of whiskey at his feet
And a barrel of porter at his head.

3. His friends assembled at the wake,
And Mrs. Finnegan called for lunch.
First they brought in tay and cake,
Then pipes, tobacco, and whiskey punch.
Biddy O'Brien began to cry,
"Such a nice clean corpse did you ever see?
Oh, Tim, mavourneen, why did you die?"
"Arragh, hold your gob," said Paddy McGhee.

4. Then Maggie O'Connor took up the job,
"Oh, Biddy," says she, "you're wrong, I'm sure."
Biddy, she gave her a belt in the gob
And left her sprawlin' on the floor.
And then the war did soon engage,
'Twas woman to woman and man to man.
Shillelagh law was all the rage,
And a row and a ruction soon began.

5. Then Mickey Maloney ducked his head
When a noggin of whiskey flew at him.
It missed, and falling on the bed,
The liquor scattered over Tim!
The corpse revives; see how he rises!
Timothy, rising from the bed,
Said, "Whirl your whiskey around like blazes,
Thanum an Dhul! Do you think I'm dead?"

The Galway Piper

Irish Folk Song

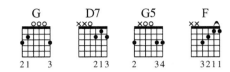

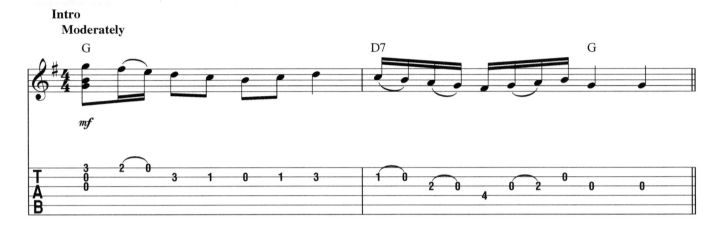

Strum Pattern: 3
Pick Pattern: 3

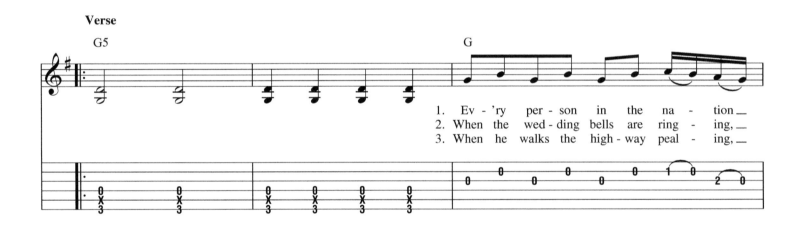

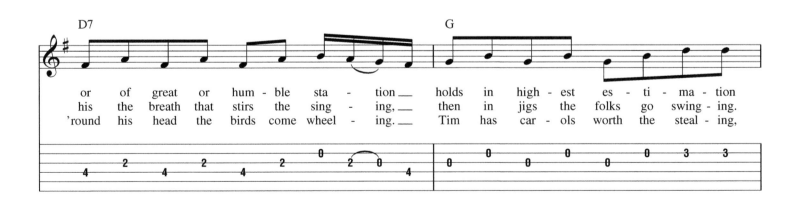

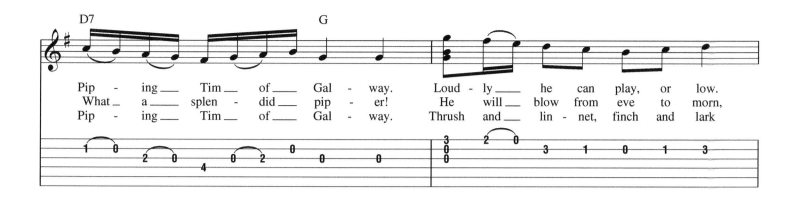

Piping ___ Tim ___ of ___ Gal - way. Loud - ly ___ he can play, or low.
What ___ a ___ splen - did ___ pip - er! He will ___ blow from eve to morn,
Pip - ing ___ Tim ___ of ___ Gal - way. Thrush and ___ lin - net, finch and lark

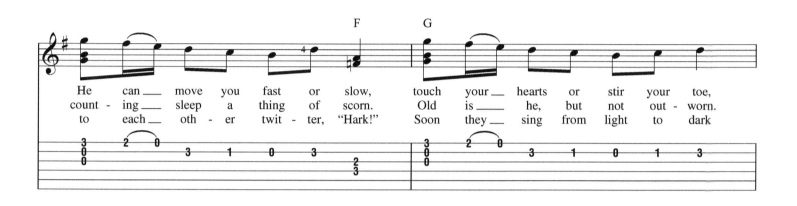

He can ___ move you fast or slow, touch your ___ hearts or stir your toe,
count - ing ___ sleep a thing of scorn. Old is ___ he, but not out - worn.
to each ___ oth - er twit - ter, "Hark!" Soon they ___ sing from light to dark

1., 2.   **3.**

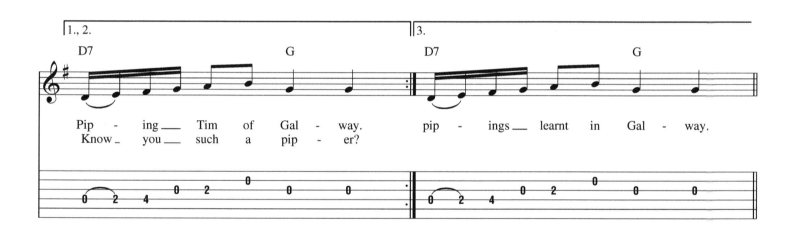

Pip - ing ___ Tim of Gal - way.   pip - ings ___ learnt in Gal - way.
Know ___ you ___ such a pip - er?

Outro

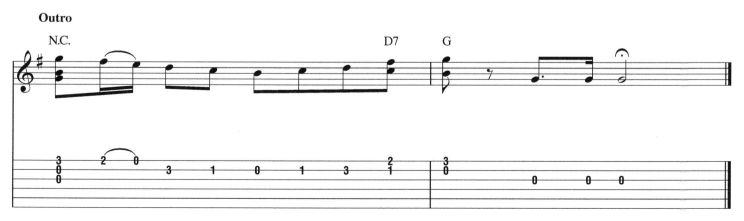

Girl I Left Behind Me

Traditional Irish

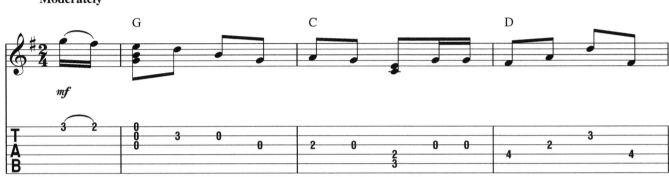

Strum Pattern: 10
Pick Pattern: 10

Intro
Moderately

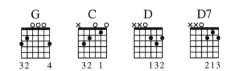

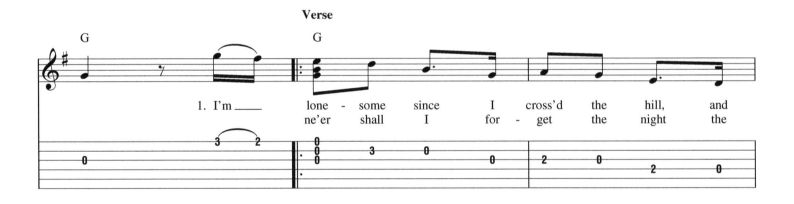

1. I'm ___ lone - some since I cross'd the hill, and
   ne'er shall I for - get the night and the

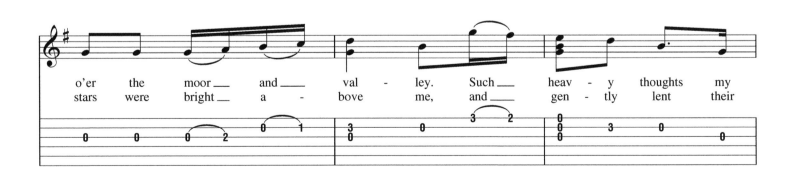

o'er the moor ___ and ___ val - ley. Such ___ heav - y thoughts my
stars were bright ___ a - bove me, and ___ gen - tly lent their

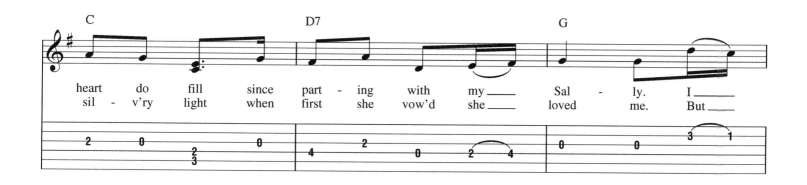

heart do fill since part - ing with my _____ Sal - ly. I _____
sil - v'ry light since when first she vow'd she _____ loved me. But _____

seek no more the fine and gay, for each does but re -
now I'm more bound to Brigh - ton Camp, kind heav'n may fa - vor

mind me how _____ swift the hours did pass a - way with the
find me, and _____ send me safe - ly back a - gain to the

girl I left be - hind me.
girl I left be - hind me.

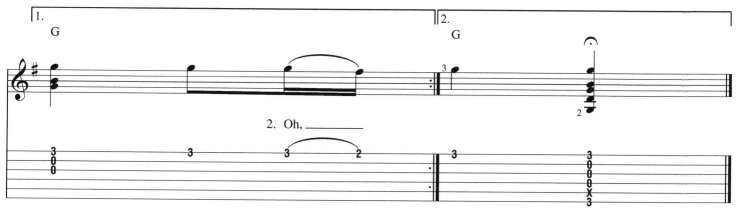

1.
G

2.
G

2. Oh, _____

I Know My Love

Traditional Irish Folk Song

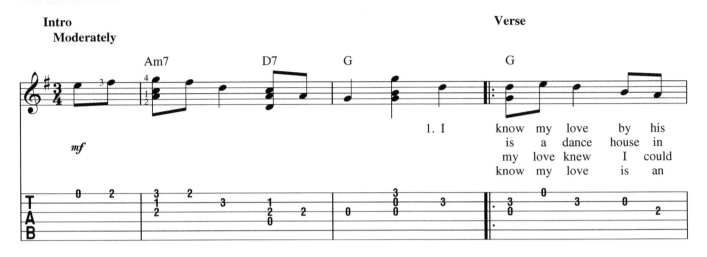

Strum Pattern: 8
Pick Pattern: 8

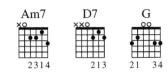

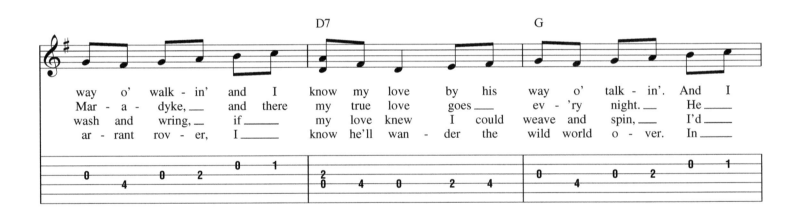

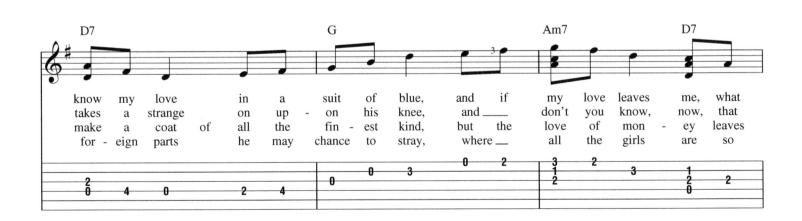

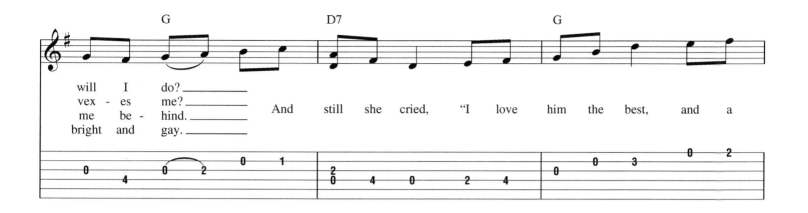

will   I   do? _____
vex - es   me? _____   And   still   she   cried,   "I   love   him   the   best,   and   a
me   be - hind. _____
bright   and   gay. _____

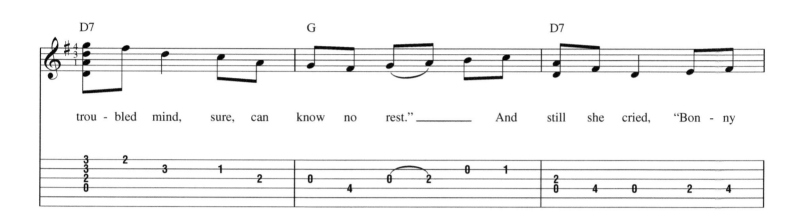

trou - bled   mind,   sure,   can   know   no   rest." _____   And   still   she   cried,   "Bon - ny

boys   are   few,   and   if   my   love   leaves   me,   what   will   I   do?"

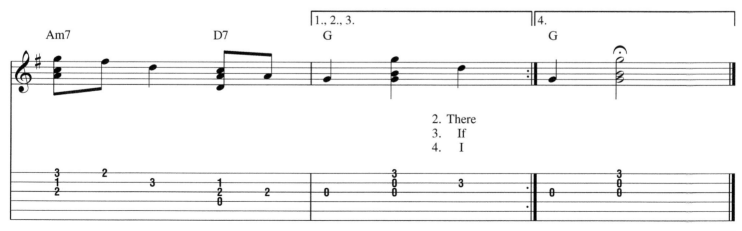

1., 2., 3.   4.

2. There
3. If
4. I

I'll Tell Me Ma

Traditional Irish Folk Song

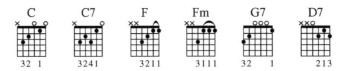

Strum Pattern: 4
Pick Pattern: 4

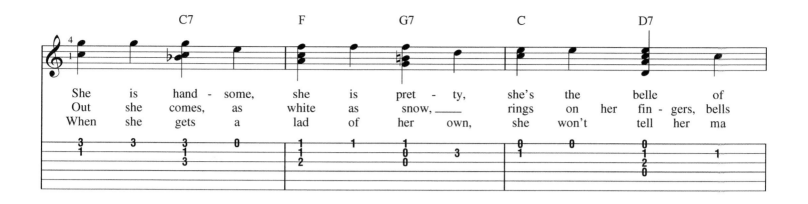

She is hand - some, she is pret - ty, she's the belle of
Out she comes, as white as snow, ____ rings on her fin - gers, bells
When she gets a lad of her own, she won't tell her ma

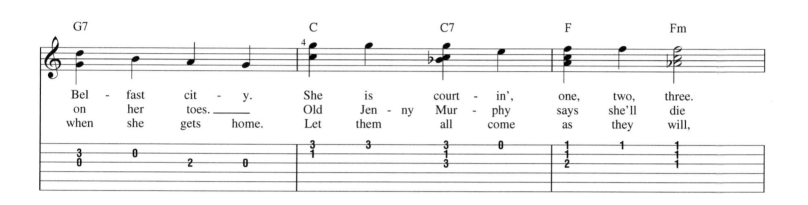

Bel - fast cit - y. She is court - in', one, two, three.
on her toes. ____ Old Jen - ny Mur - phy says she'll die
when she gets home. Let them all come as they will,

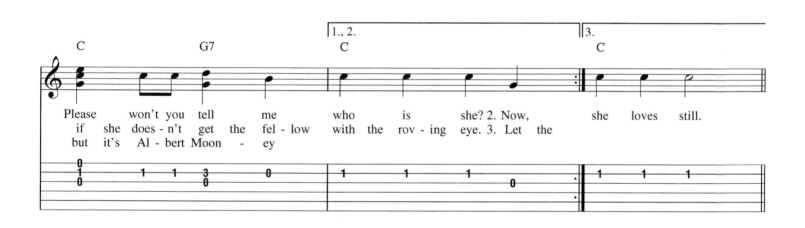

Please won't you tell me who is she? 2. Now, she loves still.
if she does - n't get the fel - low with the rov - ing eye. 3. Let the
but it's Al - bert Moon - ey

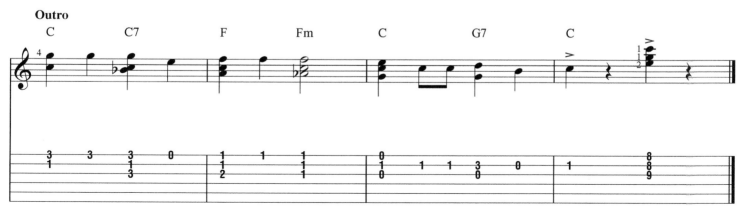

Outro

Johnny, I Hardly Knew You

Traditional Irish Folk Song

Strum Pattern: 8
Pick Pattern: 8

Intro
Moderately, in 2

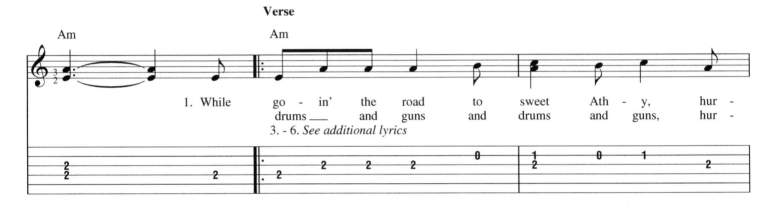

Verse

1. While go - in' the road to sweet Ath - y, hur -
drums ___ and guns and sweet drums and guns, hur -
3. - 6. See additional lyrics

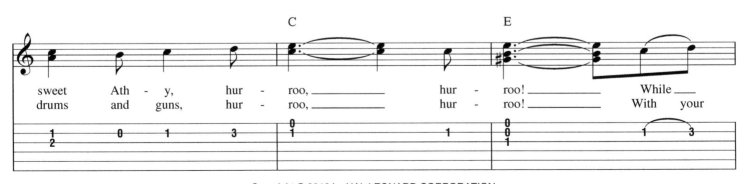

roo, _____ hur - roo! _____ While go - in' the road to
roo, _____ hur - roo! _____ With your drums ___ and guns and

sweet Ath - y, hur - roo, _____ hur - roo! _____ While ___
drums and guns, hur - roo, _____ hur - roo! _____ With your

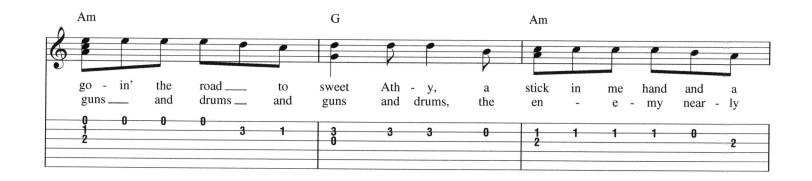

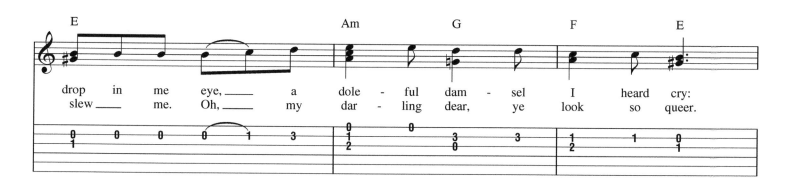

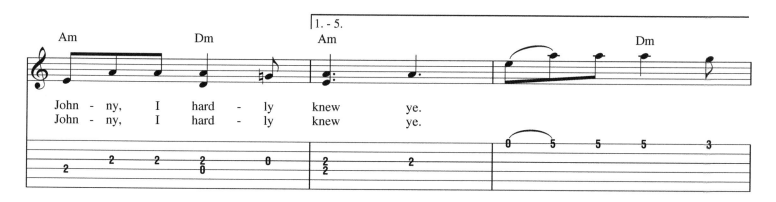

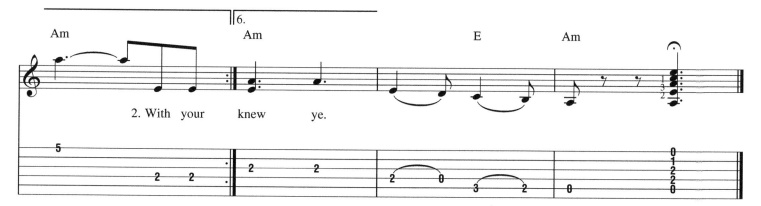

Additional Lyrics

3. Where are your eyes that were so mild, hurroo, hurroo!
   Where are your eyes that were so mild, hurroo, hurroo!
   Where are your eyes that were so mild
   When my heart you so beguiled?
   Why did ye run from me and the child?
   Johnny, I hardly knew ye.

4. Where are your legs that used to run, hurroo, hurroo!
   Where are your legs that used to run, hurroo, hurroo!
   Where are your legs that used to run
   When you went for to carry a gun?
   Indeed your dancing days are done.
   Johnny, I hardly knew ye.

5. I'm happy for to see you home, hurroo, hurroo!
   I'm happy for to see you home, hurroo, hurroo!
   I'm happy for to see you home
   All from the island of Sulloon,
   So low in flesh, so high in bone.
   Johnny, I hardly knew ye.

6. Ye haven't an arm, ye haven't a leg, hurroo, hurroo!
   Ye haven't an arm, ye haven't a leg, hurroo, hurroo!
   Ye haven't an arm, ye haven't a leg,
   Ye're an armless, boneless, chickenless egg.
   Ye'll have to put with a bowl out to beg.
   Johnny, I hardly knew ye.

The Jolly Beggarman

Traditional Irish Folk Song

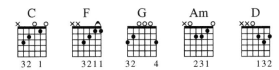

Strum Pattern: 3
Pick Pattern: 3

Intro
Fast

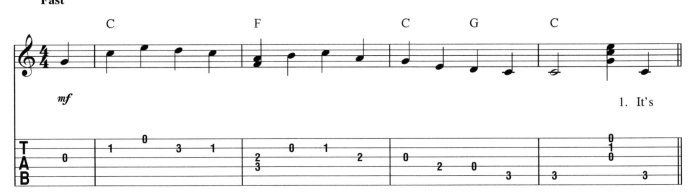

Verse

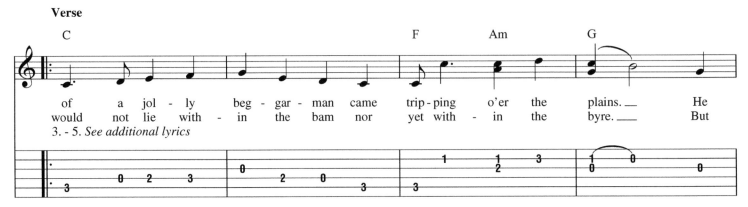

of a jol - ly beg - gar - man came trip - ping o'er the plains. __ He
would not lie with - in the barn nor yet with - in the byre. __ But

3. - 5. See additional lyrics

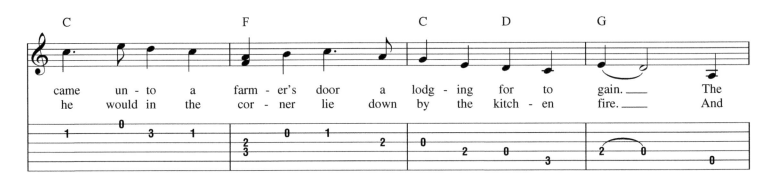

came un - to a farm - er's door a lodg - ing for to gain. __ The
he would in the cor - ner lie down by the kitch - en fire. __ And

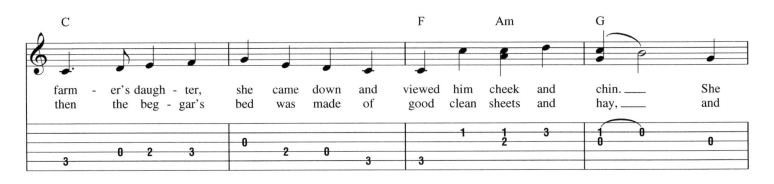

farm - er's daugh - ter, she came down and viewed him cheek and chin. __ She
then the beg - gar's bed was made of good clean sheets and hay, __ and

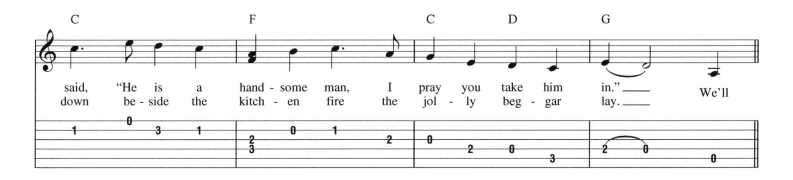

said, "He is a hand - some man, I pray you take him in." _____ We'll
down be - side the kitch - en fire the jol - ly beg - gar lay. _____

Chorus

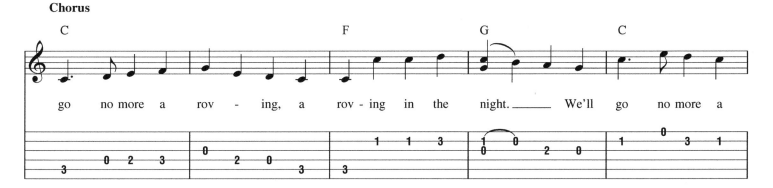

go no more a rov - ing, a rov - ing in the night._____ We'll go no more a

1. - 4.

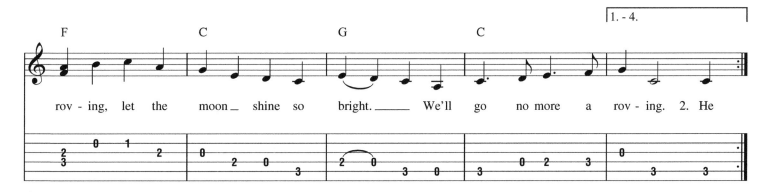

rov - ing, let the moon _ shine so bright. _____ We'll go no more a rov - ing. 2. He

5. **Outro**

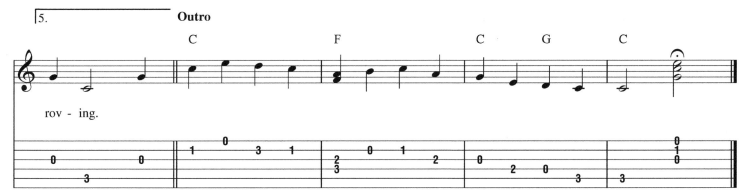

rov - ing.

Additional Lyrics

3. "O farmer's daughter, she got up to bolt the kitchen door.
And there she saw the beggar standing naked on the floor.
He took the daughter in his arms and to the bed he ran.
"Kind Sir," she said, "Be easy now, you'll waken our good man."

4. "O no, you are no beggar man, you are some gentleman,
For you have stole my maidenhead and I am quite undone."
"I am no lord, I am no squire, of beggars I be one,
And beggars, they be robbers all and you are quite undone."

5. The farmer's wife came down the stairs, awakened from her sleep.
She saw the beggar and the girl and she began to weep.
She took the bed in both her hands and threw it at the wall,
Saying, "Go you with the beggarman, your maidenhead and all!"

Kitty of Coleraine

Irish Folk Song

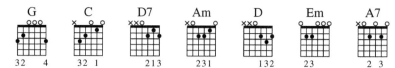

Strum Pattern: 8
Pick Pattern: 8

Intro
Moderately fast

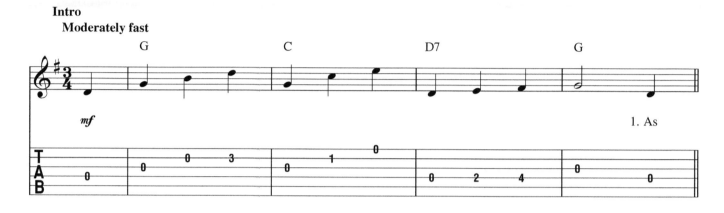

1. As

Verse

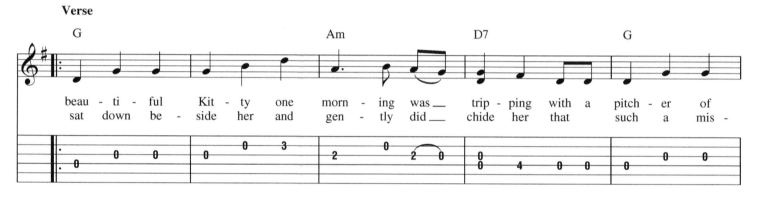

beau - ti - ful Kit - ty one morn - ing was __ trip - ping with a pitch - er of
sat down be - side her and gen - tly did __ chide her that such a mis -

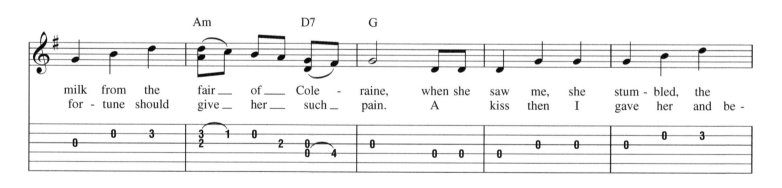

milk from the fair __ of __ Cole - raine, when she saw me, she stum - bled, the
for - tune should give __ her __ such __ pain. A kiss then I gave her and be -

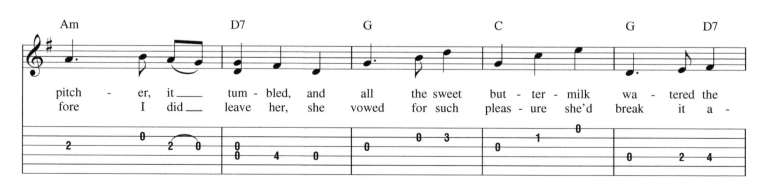

pitch - er, it ____ tum - bled, and all the sweet but - ter - milk wa - tered the
fore I did ____ leave her, she vowed for such pleas - ure she'd break it a -

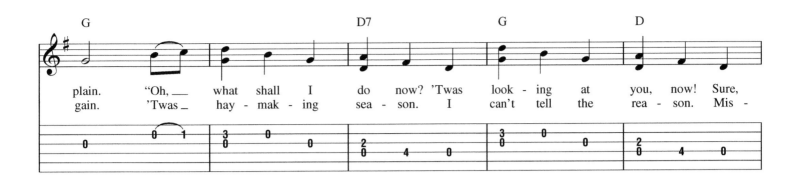

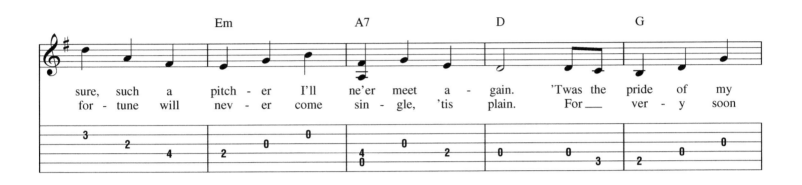

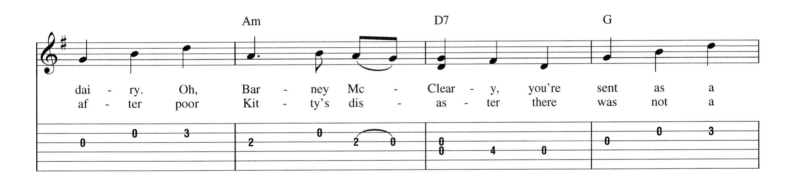

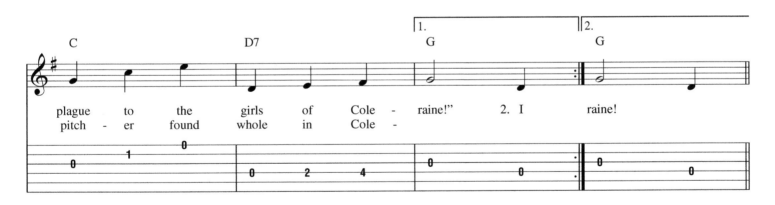

Outro

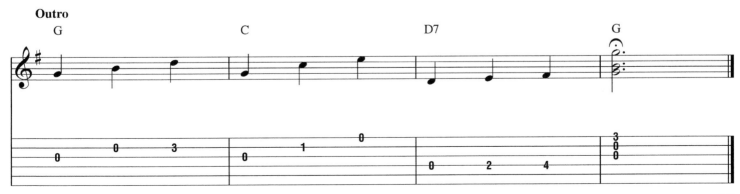

Lanigan's Ball

Traditional Irish Folk Song

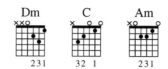

Strum Pattern: 3
Pick Pattern: 3

Intro
Moderately, in 2

1. In the

Verse

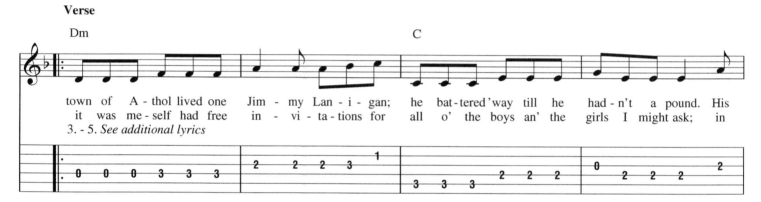

town of A - thol lived one Jim - my Lan - i - gan; he bat - tered 'way till he had - n't a pound. His
it was me - self had free in - vi - ta - tions for all o' the boys an' the girls I might ask; in
3. - 5. *See additional lyrics*

fa - ther, he died and made him a man a - gain; left him a farm of ten a - cres of ground.
less that five min - utes I'd friends and re - la - tions all sing - ing as mer - ry as flies 'round a cask.

He gave a large par - ty to all his re - la - tions that stood be - side him when he
Now Kit - ty O' - Ha - ra, a nate lit - tle mil - li - ner, tipt me the wink and then

Additional Lyrics

3. The boys were all merry, the girls were frisky,
   All drinking together in couples and groups,
   Till an accident happened to Paddy O'Rafferty,
   He stuck his foot through Miss Flanigan's hoops.
   The creature, she fainted and roared, "Millia murther!"
   Then called for her friends and gathered them all.
   Tim Dermody swore that he'd go no further,
   But have satisfaction at Lanigan's Ball.

4. Oh, arragh, boys, but then was the ruction;
   Meself got a wollop from Phelim McCoo.
   Soon, I replied to his nate introduction
   And we kicked up the divil's own phililaloo.
   Casey, the piper, he was nearly strangled;
   He squeezed up his bags, chaunters and all.
   The girls in their ribbons all got entangled,
   And that put a stop to Lanigan's Ball.

5. In the midst of the row, Miss Kavanagh fainted;
   Her face all the while was as red as the rose.
   The ladies declared her cheeks they were painted,
   But she'd taken a drop too much, I suppose.
   Paddy McCarty, so hearty and able,
   When he saw his dear colleen stretched out in the hall,
   He pulled the best leg from out under the table
   And broke all the chiney at Lanigan's Ball.

The Lark in the Clear Air

Words and Music by Sir Samuel Ferguson

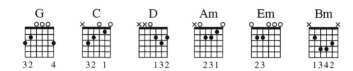

Strum Pattern: 9
Pick Pattern: 9

Intro
Moderately

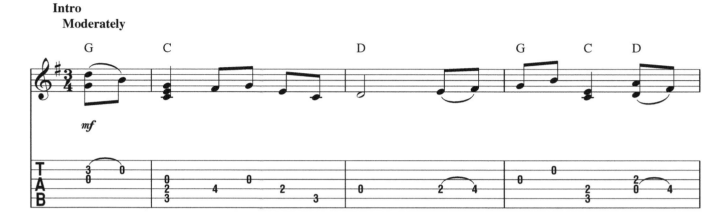

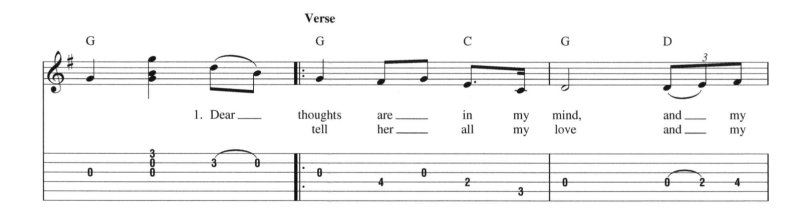

1. Dear ____ thoughts are ____ in my mind, and ____ my
   tell her ____ all my love and ____ my

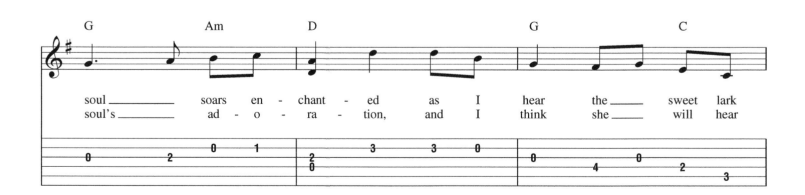

soul ____ soars en - chant - ed as I hear the ____ sweet lark
soul's ____ ad - o - ra - tion, and I think she ____ will hear

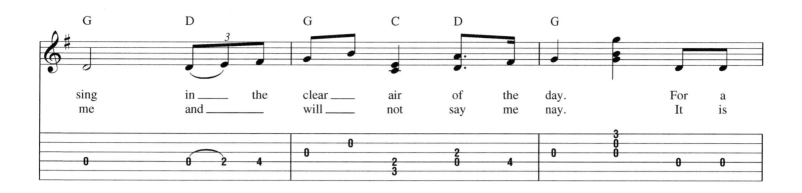

sing in the clear air of the day. For a
me and will not say me nay. It is

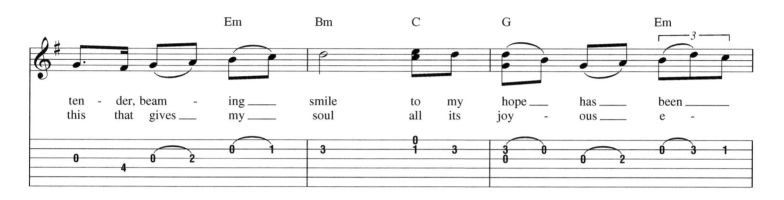

ten - der, beam - ing smile to my hope has been
this that gives my soul all its joy - ous e -

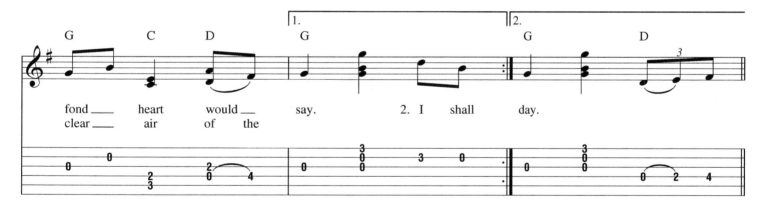

grant - ed, and to - mor - row she shall hear all my
la - tion as I hear the sweet lark sing in the

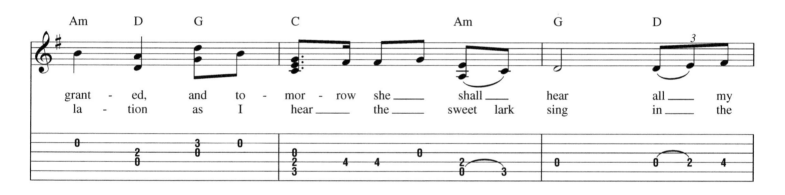

fond heart would say. 2. I shall day.
clear air of the

Outro

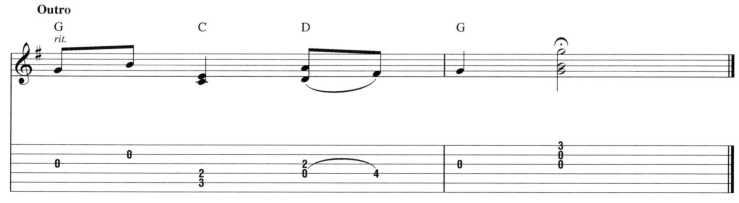

Let Erin Remember the Days of Old

Lyrics by Thomas Moore
Folk Melody "The Red Fox"

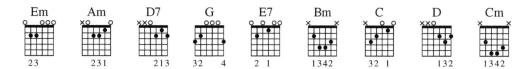

Strum Pattern: 3
Pick Pattern: 3

Intro
Moderately slow

mf

1. Let

Verse

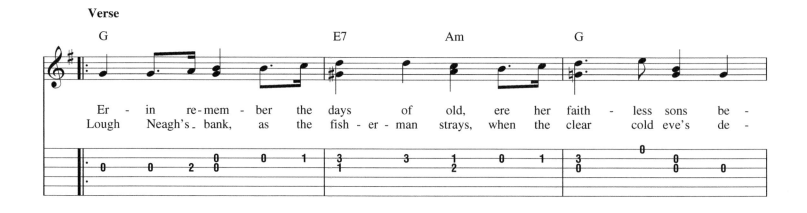

Er - in re-mem - ber the days of old, ere her faith - less sons be -
Lough Neagh's bank, as the fish - er - man strays, when the clear cold eve's de -

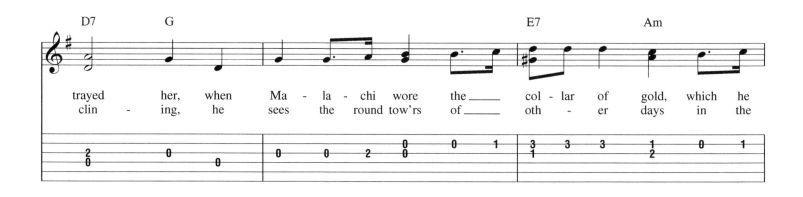

trayed her, when Ma - la - chi wore the ___ col - lar of gold, which he
clin - ing, he sees the round tow'rs of ___ oth - er days in the

Loch Lomond

Scottish Folksong

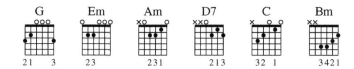

Strum Pattern: 3
Pick Pattern: 4

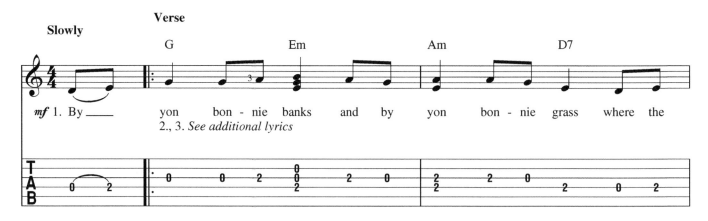

By ____ yon bon - nie banks and by yon bon - nie grass where the

2., 3. *See additional lyrics*

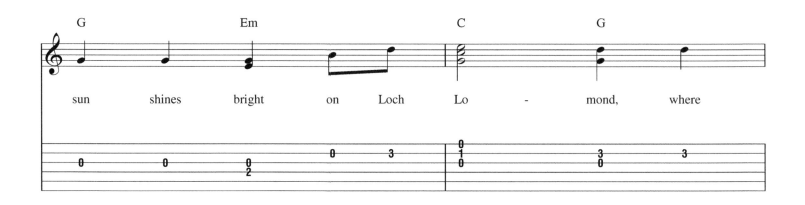

sun shines bright on Loch Lo - mond, where

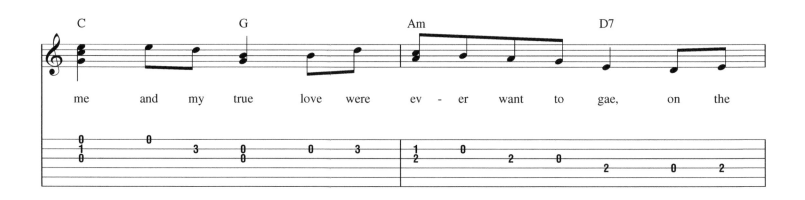

me and my true love were ev - er want to gae, on the

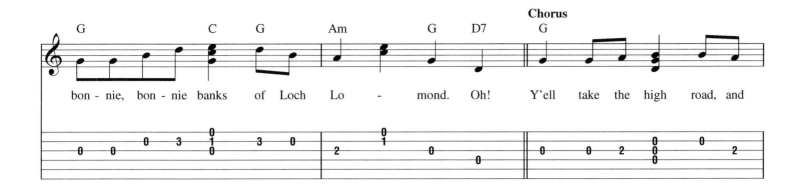

bon - nie, bon - nie banks of Loch Lo - mond. Oh! Y'ell take the high road, and

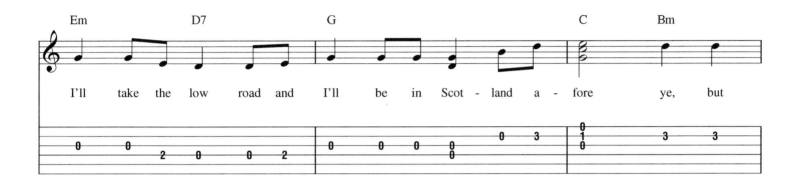

I'll take the low road and I'll be in Scot - land a - fore ye, but

me and ny true love, we'll nev - er meet a - gain on the

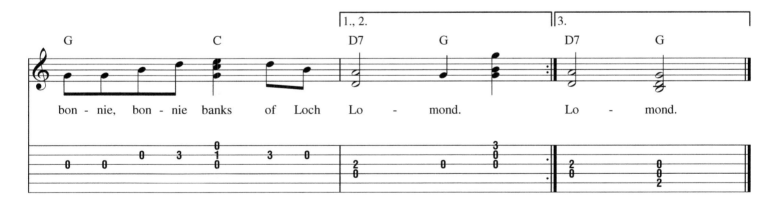

bon - nie, bon - nie banks of Loch Lo - mond. Lo - mond.

Additional Lyrics

2. 'Twas then that we parted in yon shady glen,
   On the steep, steep side of Ben Lomond.
   Where in purple hue, the Highland hills we view
   And the moon coming out in the gloaming.

3. The wee birdies sing, and the wildflowers spring,
   And in sunshine, the waters are sleeping.
   But the broken heart, it kens, nae second spring again,
   Tho' the woeful may cease their greeting.

Minstrel Boy

Traditional

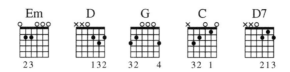

Strum Pattern: 5
Pick Pattern: 4

Intro
Moderately

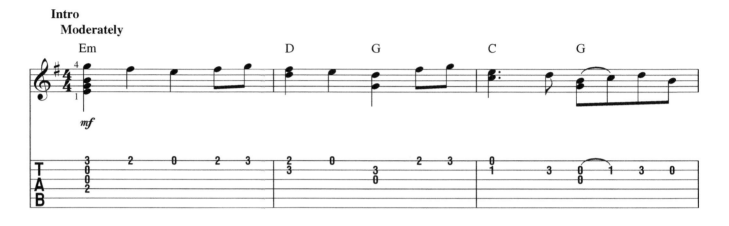

Verse

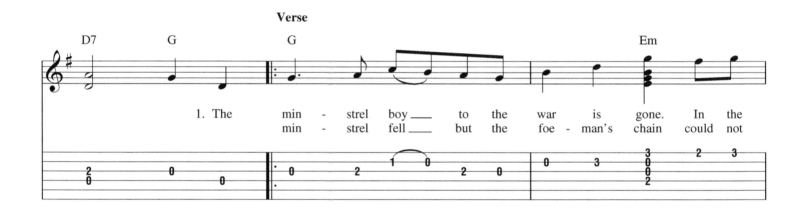

1. The min - strel boy ___ to the war is gone. In the
   min - strel fell ___ but the foe - man's chain could not

ranks of death ___ you'll find ___ him. His fa - ther's sword ___ he has
bring his proud ___ soul un - der. The harp he loved ___ nev - er

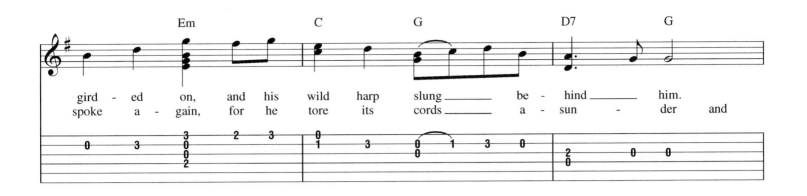

girded on, and his wild harp slung _____ be - hind _____ him.
spoke a - gain, for he tore its cords _____ a - sun - der and

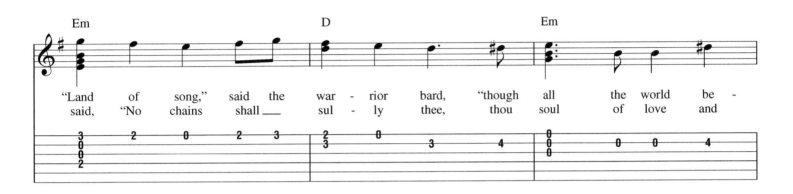

"Land of song," said the war - rior bard, "though all the world be -
said, "No chains shall ____ sul - ly thee, thou soul of love and

trays _____ thee, one sword at least ____ thy ____ rights shall guard, one ____
brav - er - y! Thy songs were made ____ for the pure and free. They shall

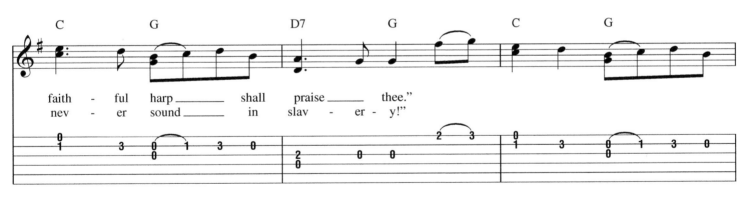

faith - ful harp _____ shall praise _____ thee."
nev - er sound _____ in slav - er - y!"

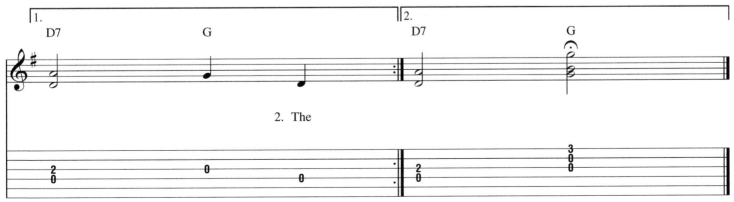

2. The

Molly Brannigan

Irish Folk Song

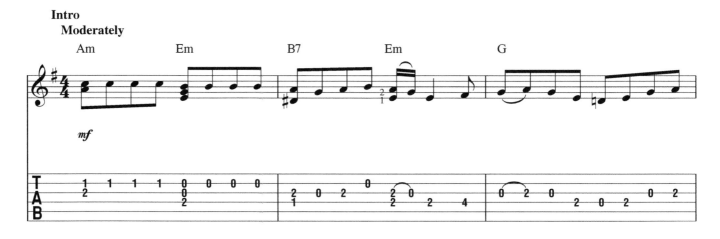

Strum Pattern: 3
Pick Pattern: 3

Intro
Moderately

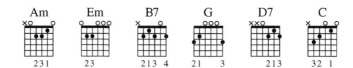

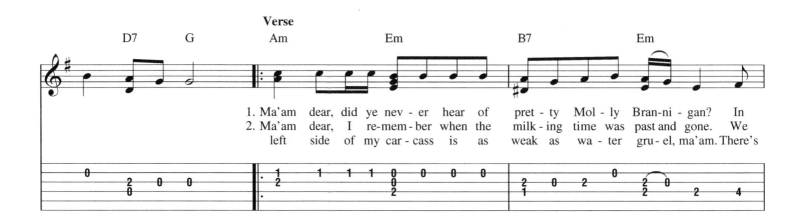

1. Ma'am dear, did ye nev - er hear of pret - ty Mol - ly Bran-ni - gan? In
2. Ma'am dear, I re-mem - ber when the milk - ing time was past and gone. We
left side of my car - cass is as weak as wa - ter gru-el, ma'am. There's

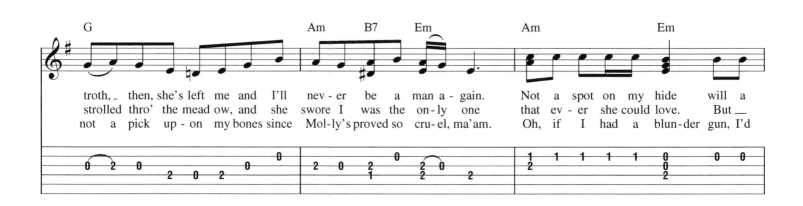

troth, _ then, she's left me and I'll nev - er be a man a - gain. Not a spot on my hide will a
strolled thro' the mead ow, and she swore I was the on-ly one that ev - er she could love. But _
not a pick up - on my bones since Mol-ly's proved so cru-el, ma'am. Oh, if I had a blun-der gun, I'd

The Mountains of Mourne

Words by Percy French
Traditional Irish Melody

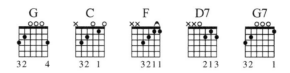

Strum Pattern: 7
Pick Pattern: 7

Intro
Moderately

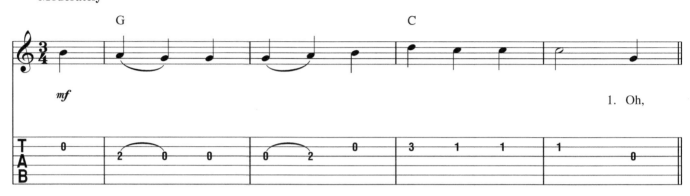

1. Oh,

Verse

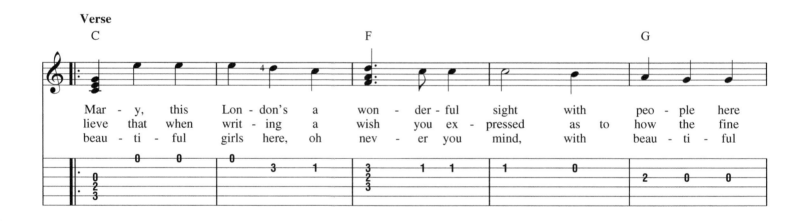

Mar - y, this Lon - don's a won - der - ful sight with peo - ple here
lieve that when writ - ing a wish you ex - pressed with as to how the here fine
beau - ti - ful girls here, oh nev - er you mind, with beau - ti - ful

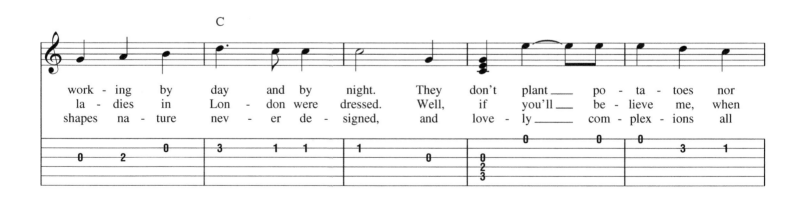

work - ing by day and by night. They don't plant po - ta - toes nor
la - dies in Lon - don were dressed. Well, if you'll be - lieve me, when
shapes na - ture nev - er de - signed, and love - ly com - plex - ions all

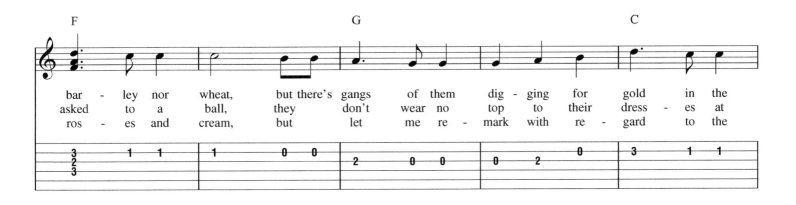

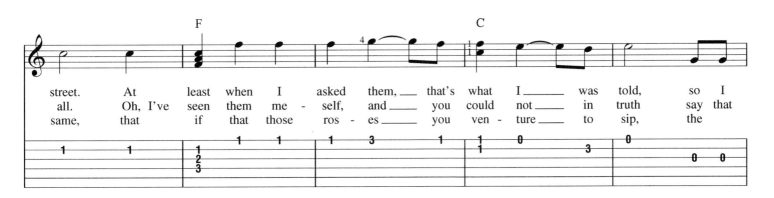

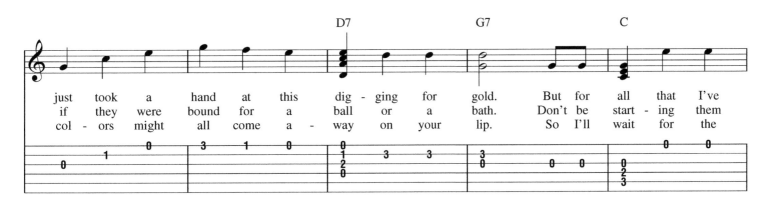

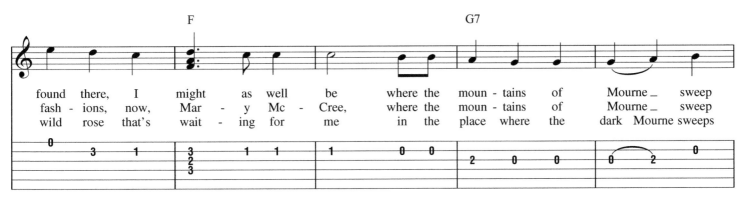

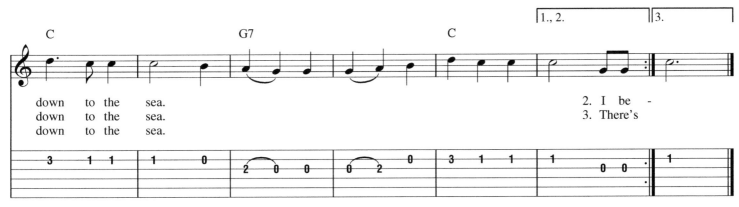

The Rising of the Moon

Traditional Irish Folk Song

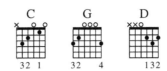

Strum Pattern: 3
Pick Pattern: 3

Intro
Moderately, in 2

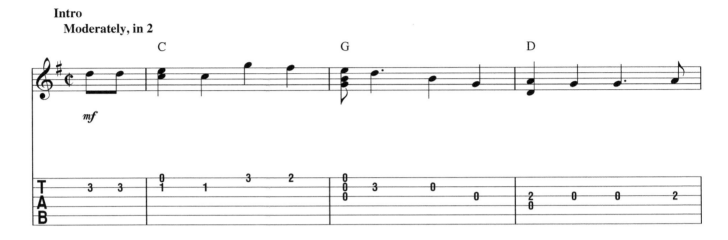

Verse

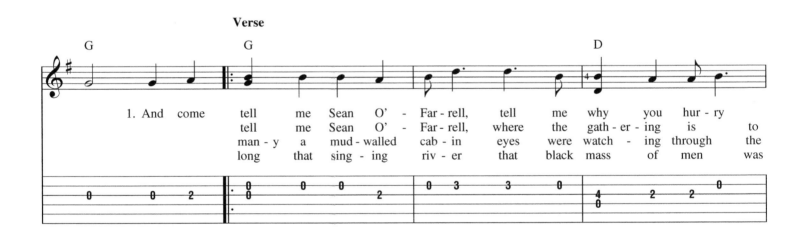

1. And come   tell   me   Sean O' - Far - rell,   tell   me   why   you   hur - ry
  tell   me   Sean O' - Far - rell,   where   the   gath - er - ing   is   to
  man - y   a   mud - walled   cab - in   eyes   were   watch - ing through   the
  long   that   sing - ing   riv - er   that   black   mass   of   men   was

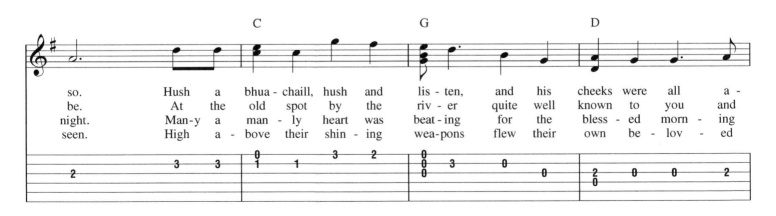

so.   Hush   a   bhua - chaill, hush   and   lis - ten,   and   his   cheeks   were   all   a -
be.   At   the   old   spot   by   the   riv - er   quite   well   known   to   you   and
night.   Man-y   a   man - ly   heart   was   beat - ing   for   the   bless - ed   morn - ing
seen.   High   a - bove   their   shin - ing   wea - pons   flew   their   own   be - lov - ed

She Moved Thro' the Fair

(She Moved Through the Fair)

Traditional Irish Melody

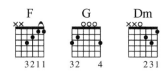

Strum Pattern: 9
Pick Pattern: 9

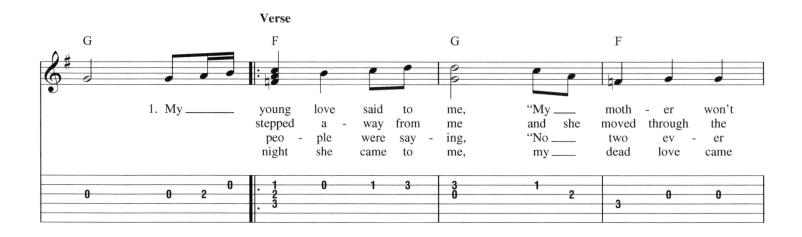

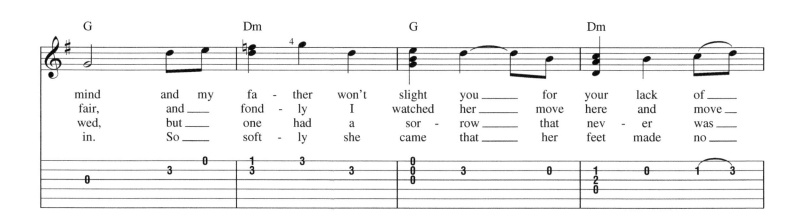

The Skye Boat Song

Traditional

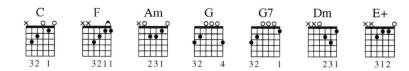

Strum Pattern: 7
Pick Pattern: 7

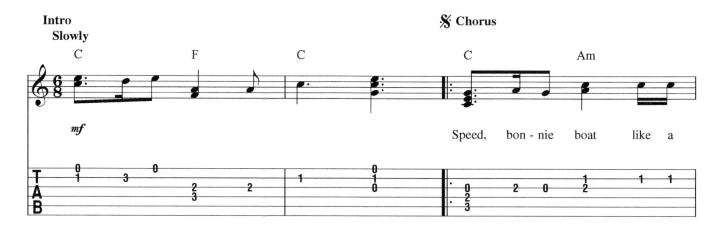

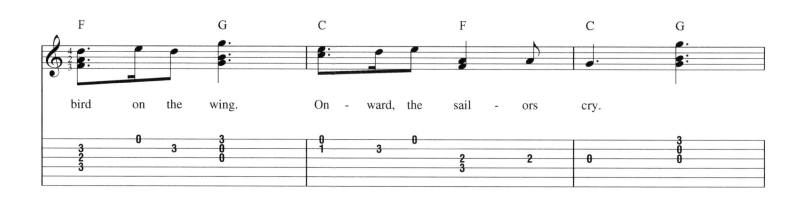

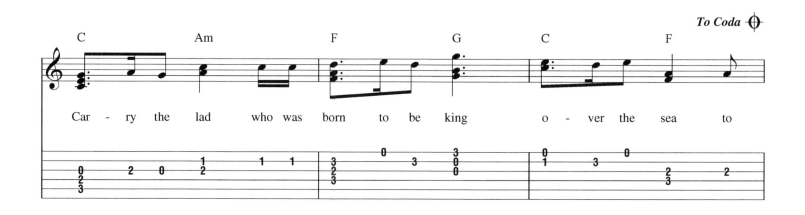

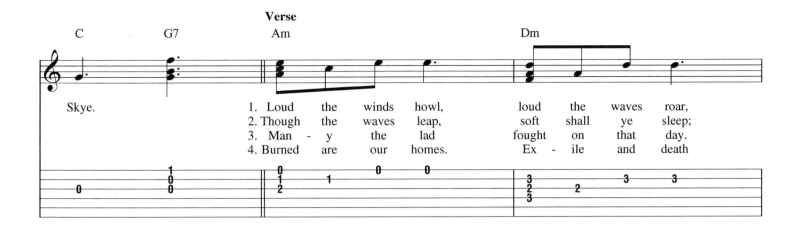

Verse

Skye.

1. Loud the winds howl, loud the waves roar,
2. Though the waves leap, soft shall ye sleep;
3. Man - y the lad fought on that day.
4. Burned are our homes. Ex - ile and death

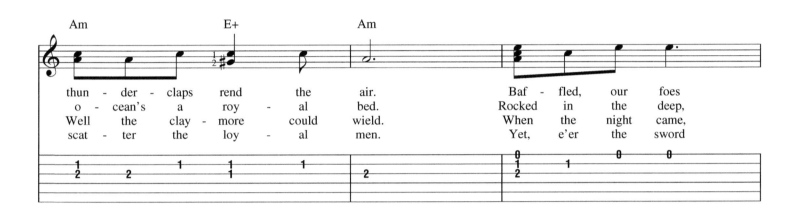

thun - der - claps rend the air. Baf - fled, our foes
o - cean's a roy - al bed. Rocked in the deep,
Well the clay - more could wield. When the night came,
scat - ter the loy - al men. Yet, e'er the sword

4th time, D.S. al Coda

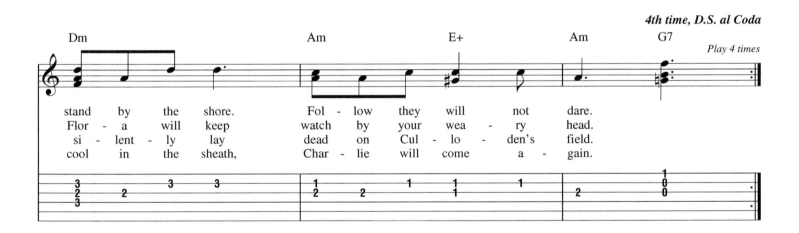

Play 4 times

stand by the shore. Fol - low they will not dare.
Flor - a will keep watch by your wea - ry head.
si - lent - ly lay dead on Cul - lo - den's field.
cool in the sheath, Char - lie will come a - gain.

Coda

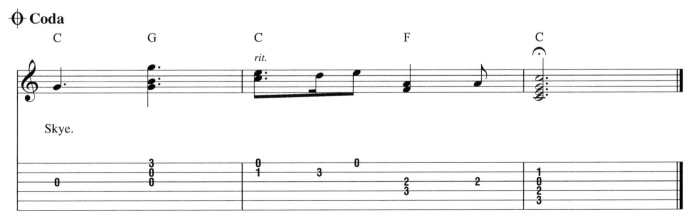

Skye.

'Tis the Last Rose of Summer

Words by Thomas Moore
Music by Richard Alfred Milliken

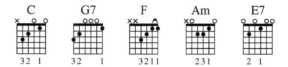

Strum Pattern: 8
Pick Pattern: 8

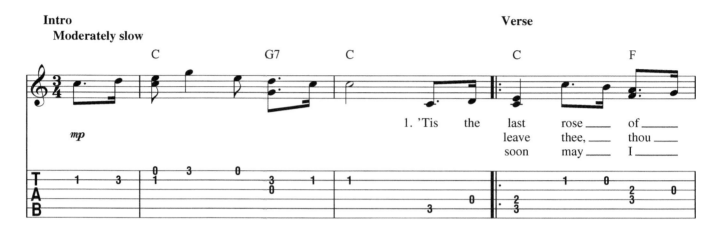

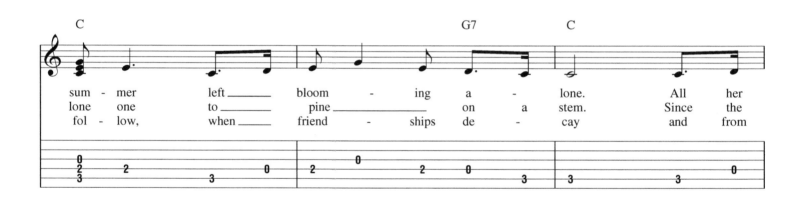

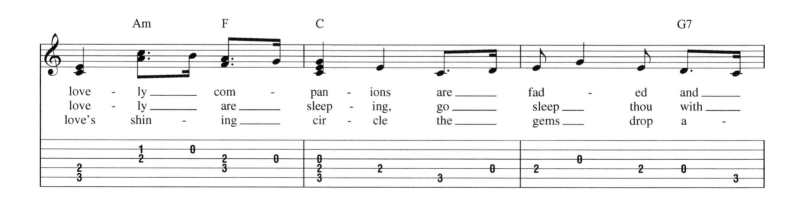

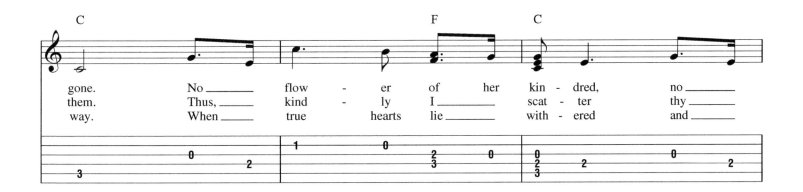

gone.   No _____ flow - er of her kin - dred,   no _____
them.   Thus, _____ kind - ly I _____ scat - ter   thy _____
way.   When _____ true hearts lie _____ with - ered   and _____

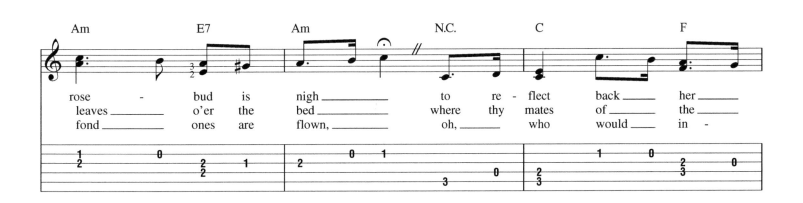

rose - bud is nigh _____ to re - flect back _____ her _____
leaves _____ o'er the bed _____ where thy mates of _____ the _____
fond _____ ones are flown, _____ oh, _____ who would ____ in -

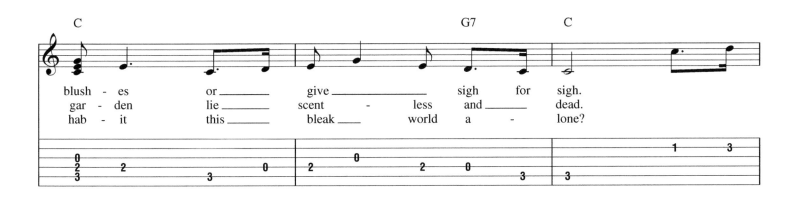

blush - es or _____ give _____ sigh for sigh.
gar - den lie _____ scent - less and _____ dead.
hab - it this _____ bleak ____ world a - lone?

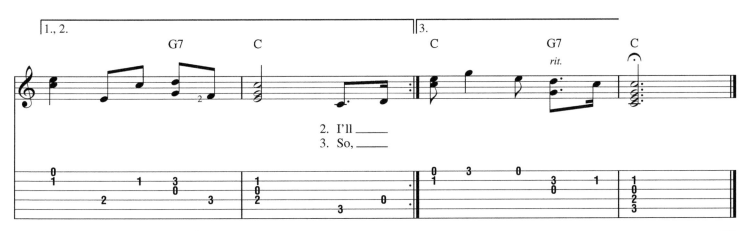

2. I'll _____
3. So, _____

Where the River Shannon Flows

By James J. Russell

Strum Pattern: 4
Pick Pattern: 4

Intro
Moderately

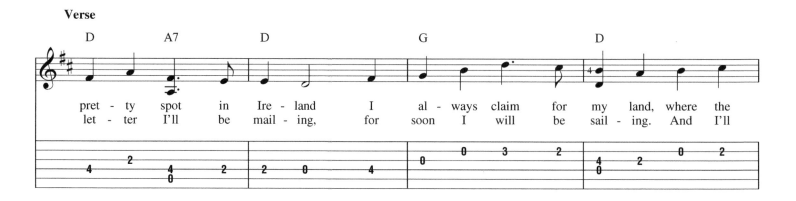

mp

1. There's a
2. Sure no

Verse

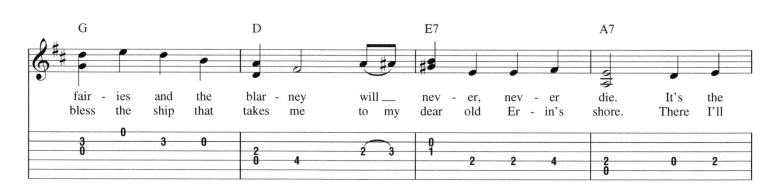

pret - ty spot in Ire - land I al - ways claim for my land, where the
let - ter I'll be mail - ing, for soon I will be sail - ing. And I'll

fair - ies and the blar - ney will __ nev - er, nev - er die. It's the
bless the ship that takes me to my dear old Er - in's shore. There I'll

land of the shil - la - lah. My heart goes back there dai - ly to the
set - tle down for - ev - er. I'll leave my old sod nev - er, and I'll

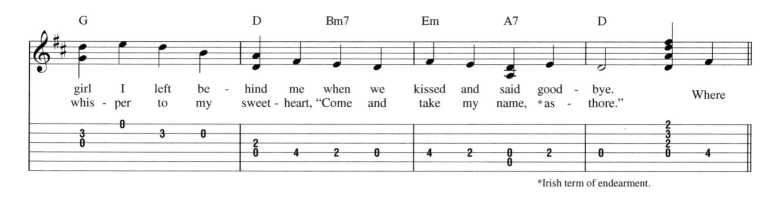

girl I left be - hind me when we kissed and said good - bye. Where
whis - per to my sweet - heart, "Come and take my name, *as - thore." Where

*Irish term of endearment.

Chorus

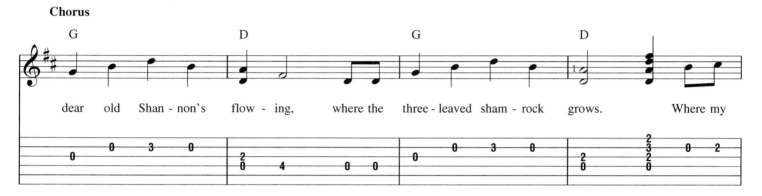

dear old Shan - non's flow - ing, where the three - leaved sham - rock grows. Where my

heart is, I am go - ing, to my lit - tle I - rish rose. And the mo - ment that I

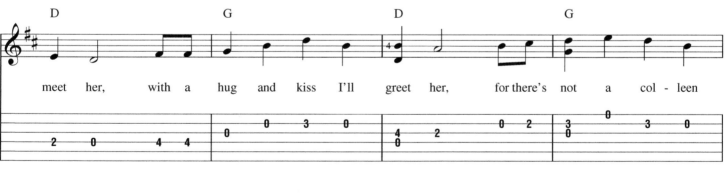

meet her, with a hug and kiss I'll greet her, for there's not a col - leen

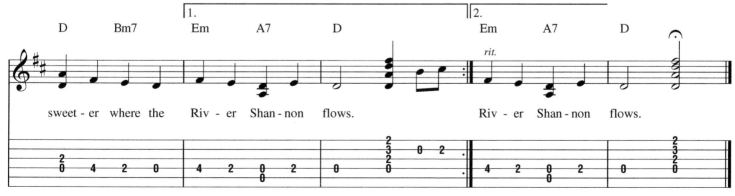

sweet - er where the Riv - er Shan - non flows. Riv - er Shan - non flows.

Rory O'Moore

Traditional Irish Folk Song

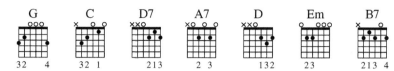

Strum Pattern: 8
Pick Pattern: 8

Intro
Moderately, in 2

Verse

1. Young Ror - y O' - Moore court - ed Kath - a - leen Bawn. He was
deed then," says Kath - leen, "don't think of the like, for I
Kath - leen, my dar - ling, you've teaz'd me e - nough, and I've

bold as a hawk, and she soft as the dawn. He
half gave a prom - ise she to sooth - er - ing Mike. The
thrash'd for your sake Din - ny Grimes and Jim Duff. And I've

wish'd in his heart pret - ty Kath - leen to please, and he
ground that I walk on he loves, I'll be bound." "Faith," says
made my - self drink - ing your health quite a baste, so I

Jew - el," says Ror - y, "that same is the way you've
Jew - el, keep dream - ing that same till you die, and you've
Ror - y, leave off, sir, you'll hug me no more, that's

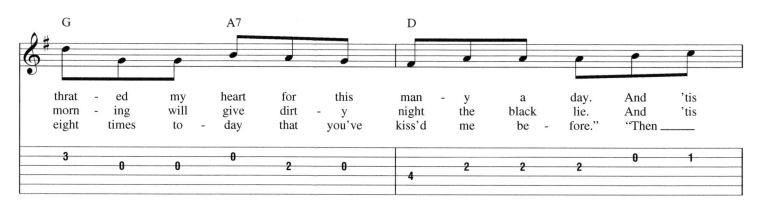

thrat - ed my heart for this man - y a day. And 'tis
morn - ing will give dirt - y night the black lie. And 'tis
eight times to - day that you've kiss'd me be - fore." "Then _____

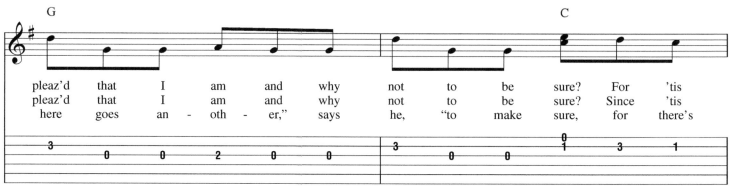

pleaz'd that I am and why not to be sure? For 'tis
pleaz'd that I am and why not to be sure? Since 'tis
here goes an - oth - er," says he, "to make sure, for there's

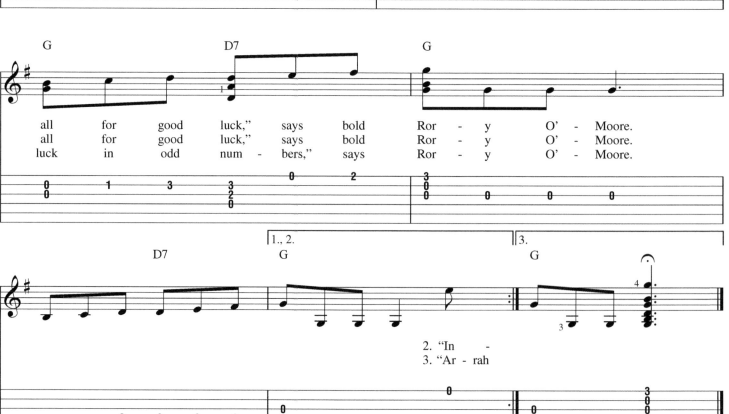

all for good luck," says bold Ror - y O' - Moore.
all for good luck," says bold Ror - y O' - Moore.
luck in odd num - bers," says Ror - y O' - Moore.

1., 2.

3.

2. "In -
3. "Ar - rah

EASY GUITAR
WITH NOTES & TAB

This series features simplified arrangements with notes, tab, chord charts, and strum and pick patterns.

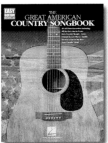  

MIXED FOLIOS

00702287	Acoustic	$19.99
00702002	Acoustic Rock Hits for Easy Guitar	$15.99
00702166	All-Time Best Guitar Collection	$19.99
00702232	Best Acoustic Songs for Easy Guitar	$16.99
00119835	Best Children's Songs	$16.99
00703055	The Big Book of Nursery Rhymes & Children's Songs	$16.99
00698978	Big Christmas Collection	$19.99
00702394	Bluegrass Songs for Easy Guitar	$15.99
00289632	Bohemian Rhapsody	$19.99
00703387	Celtic Classics	$14.99
00224808	Chart Hits of 2016-2017	$14.99
00267383	Chart Hits of 2017-2018	$14.99
00334293	Chart Hits of 2019-2020	$16.99
00702149	Children's Christian Songbook	$9.99
00702028	Christmas Classics	$8.99
00101779	Christmas Guitar	$14.99
00702141	Classic Rock	$8.95
00159642	Classical Melodies	$12.99
00253933	Disney/Pixar's Coco	$16.99
00702203	CMT's 100 Greatest Country Songs	$34.99
00702283	The Contemporary Christian Collection	$16.99
00196954	Contemporary Disney	$19.99
00702239	Country Classics for Easy Guitar	$24.99

00702257	Easy Acoustic Guitar Songs	$16.99
00702041	Favorite Hymns for Easy Guitar	$12.99
00222701	Folk Pop Songs	$17.99
00126894	Frozen	$14.99
00333922	Frozen 2	$14.99
00702286	Glee	$16.99
00702160	The Great American Country Songbook	$19.99
00702148	Great American Gospel for Guitar	$14.99
00702050	Great Classical Themes for Easy Guitar	$9.99
00275088	The Greatest Showman	$17.99
00148030	Halloween Guitar Songs	$14.99
00702273	Irish Songs	$12.99
00192503	Jazz Classics for Easy Guitar	$16.99
00702275	Jazz Favorites for Easy Guitar	$17.99
00702274	Jazz Standards for Easy Guitar	$19.99
00702162	Jumbo Easy Guitar Songbook	$24.99
00232285	La La Land	$16.99
00702258	Legends of Rock	$14.99
00702189	MTV's 100 Greatest Pop Songs	$34.99
00702272	1950s Rock	$16.99
00702271	1960s Rock	$16.99
00702270	1970s Rock	$19.99
00702269	1980s Rock	$15.99
00702268	1990s Rock	$19.99
00369043	Rock Songs for Kids	$14.99

00109725	Once	$14.99
00702187	Selections from O Brother Where Art Thou?	$19.99
00702178	100 Songs for Kids	$14.99
00702515	Pirates of the Caribbean	$17.99
00702125	Praise and Worship for Guitar	$14.99
00287930	Songs from *A Star Is Born, The Greatest Showman, La La Land*, and More Movie Musicals	$16.99
00702285	Southern Rock Hits	$12.99
00156420	Star Wars Music	$16.99
00121535	30 Easy Celtic Guitar Solos	$16.99
00702156	3-Chord Rock	$12.99
00244654	Top Hits of 2017	$14.99
00283786	Top Hits of 2018	$14.99
00702294	Top Worship Hits	$17.99
00702255	VH1's 100 Greatest Hard Rock Songs	$34.99
00702175	VH1's 100 Greatest Songs of Rock and Roll	$29.99
00702253	Wicked	$12.99

ARTIST COLLECTIONS

00702267	AC/DC for Easy Guitar	$16.99
00702598	Adele for Easy Guitar	$15.99
00156221	Adele – 25	$16.99
00702040	Best of the Allman Brothers	$16.99
00702865	J.S. Bach for Easy Guitar	$15.99
00702169	Best of The Beach Boys	$15.99
00702292	The Beatles — 1	$22.99
00125796	Best of Chuck Berry	$15.99
00702201	The Essential Black Sabbath	$15.99
00702250	blink-182 — Greatest Hits	$17.99
02501615	Zac Brown Band — The Foundation	$17.99
02501621	Zac Brown Band — You Get What You Give	$16.99
00702043	Best of Johnny Cash	$17.99
00702090	Eric Clapton's Best	$16.99
00702086	Eric Clapton — from the Album Unplugged	$17.99
00702202	The Essential Eric Clapton	$17.99
00702053	Best of Patsy Cline	$15.99
00222697	Very Best of Coldplay – 2nd Edition	$16.99
00702229	The Very Best of Creedence Clearwater Revival	$16.99
00702145	Best of Jim Croce	$16.99
00702278	Crosby, Stills & Nash	$12.99
14042809	Bob Dylan	$15.99
00702276	Fleetwood Mac — Easy Guitar Collection	$17.99
00139462	The Very Best of Grateful Dead	$16.99
00702136	Best of Merle Haggard	$16.99
00702227	Jimi Hendrix — Smash Hits	$19.99
00702288	Best of Hillsong United	$12.99
00702236	Best of Antonio Carlos Jobim	$15.99
00702245	Elton John — Greatest Hits 1970–2002	$19.99

00129855	Jack Johnson	$16.99
00702204	Robert Johnson	$14.99
00702234	Selections from Toby Keith — 35 Biggest Hits	$12.95
00702003	Kiss	$16.99
00702216	Lynyrd Skynyrd	$16.99
00702182	The Essential Bob Marley	$16.99
00146081	Maroon 5	$14.99
00121925	Bruno Mars – Unorthodox Jukebox	$12.99
00702248	Paul McCartney — All the Best	$14.99
00125484	The Best of MercyMe	$12.99
00702209	Steve Miller Band — Young Hearts (Greatest Hits)	$12.95
00124167	Jason Mraz	$15.99
00702096	Best of Nirvana	$16.99
00702211	The Offspring — Greatest Hits	$17.99
00138026	One Direction	$17.99
00702030	Best of Roy Orbison	$17.99
00702144	Best of Ozzy Osbourne	$14.99
00702279	Tom Petty	$17.99
00102911	Pink Floyd	$17.99
00702139	Elvis Country Favorites	$19.99
00702293	The Very Best of Prince	$19.99
00699415	Best of Queen for Guitar	$16.99
00109279	Best of R.E.M.	$14.99
00702208	Red Hot Chili Peppers — Greatest Hits	$16.99
00198960	The Rolling Stones	$17.99
00174793	The Very Best of Santana	$16.99
00702196	Best of Bob Seger	$16.99
00146046	Ed Sheeran	$15.99
00702252	Frank Sinatra — Nothing But the Best	$12.99
00702010	Best of Rod Stewart	$17.99
00702049	Best of George Strait	$17.99

00702259	Taylor Swift for Easy Guitar	$15.99
00359800	Taylor Swift – Easy Guitar Anthology	$24.99
00702260	Taylor Swift — Fearless	$14.99
00139727	Taylor Swift — 1989	$17.99
00115960	Taylor Swift — Red	$16.99
00253667	Taylor Swift — Reputation	$17.99
00702290	Taylor Swift — Speak Now	$16.99
00232849	Chris Tomlin Collection – 2nd Edition	$14.99
00702226	Chris Tomlin — See the Morning	$12.95
00148643	Train	$14.99
00702427	U2 — 18 Singles	$19.99
00702108	Best of Stevie Ray Vaughan	$17.99
00279005	The Who	$14.99
00702123	Best of Hank Williams	$15.99
00194548	Best of John Williams	$14.99
00702228	Neil Young — Greatest Hits	$17.99
00119133	Neil Young — Harvest	$14.99

Prices, contents and availability subject to change without notice.

Visit Hal Leonard online at **halleonard.com**

The **Easy Guitar Play Along®** series features streamlined transcriptions of your favorite songs. Just follow the tab, listen to the audio to hear how the guitar should sound, and then play along using the backing tracks. Playback tools are provided for slowing down the tempo without changing pitch and looping challenging parts. The melody and lyrics are included in the book so that you can sing or simply follow along.

1. ROCK CLASSICS

Jailbreak • Living After Midnight • Mississippi Queen • Rocks Off • Runnin' Down a Dream • Smoke on the Water • Strutter • Up Around the Bend.

00702560 Book/CD Pack....... $14.99

2. ACOUSTIC TOP HITS

About a Girl • I'm Yours • The Lazy Song • The Scientist • 21 Guns • Upside Down • What I Got • Wonderwall.

00702569 Book/CD Pack....... $14.99

3. ROCK HITS

All the Small Things • Best of You • Brain Stew (The Godzilla Remix) • Californication • Island in the Sun • Plush • Smells Like Teen Spirit • Use Somebody.

00702570 Book/CD Pack....... $14.99

4. ROCK 'N' ROLL

Blue Suede Shoes • I Get Around • I'm a Believer • Jailhouse Rock • Oh, Pretty Woman • Peggy Sue • Runaway • Wake Up Little Susie.

00702572 Book/CD Pack....... $14.99

6. CHRISTMAS SONGS

Have Yourself a Merry Little Christmas • A Holly Jolly Christmas • The Little Drummer Boy • Run Rudolph Run • Santa Claus Is Comin' to Town • Silver and Gold • Sleigh Ride • Winter Wonderland.

00101879 Book/CD Pack......... $14.99

7. BLUES SONGS FOR BEGINNERS

Come On (Part 1) • Double Trouble • Gangster of Love • I'm Ready • Let Me Love You Baby • Mary Had a Little Lamb • San-Ho-Zay • T-Bone Shuffle.

00103235 Book/
Online Audio..........$17.99

9.ROCK SONGS FOR BEGINNERS

Are You Gonna Be My Girl • Buddy Holly • Everybody Hurts • In Bloom • Otherside • The Rock Show • Santa Monica • When I Come Around.

00103255 Book/CD Pack.....$14.99

10. GREEN DAY

Basket Case • Boulevard of Broken Dreams • Good Riddance (Time of Your Life) • Holiday • Longview • 21 Guns • Wake Me up When September Ends • When I Come Around.

00122322 Book/CD Pack.....$14.99

11. NIRVANA

All Apologies • Come As You Are • Heart Shaped Box • Lake of Fire • Lithium • The Man Who Sold the World • Rape Me • Smells Like Teen Spirit.

00122325 Book/
Online Audio........ $17.99

13. AC/DC

Back in Black • Dirty Deeds Done Dirt Cheap • For Those About to Rock (We Salute You) • Hells Bells • Highway to Hell • Rock and Roll Ain't Noise Pollution • T.N.T. • You Shook Me All Night Long.

14042895 Book/
Online Audio........ $17.99

14. JIMI HENDRIX – SMASH HITS

All Along the Watchtower • Can You See Me • Crosstown Traffic • Fire • Foxey Lady • Hey Joe • Manic Depression • Purple Haze • Red House • Remember • Stone Free • The Wind Cries Mary.

00130591 Book/
Online Audio........$24.99

HAL•LEONARD®
www.halleonard.com

Prices, contents, and availability subject to change without notice.